Thomson Township's
NIGHT OF TERROR
The GREAT 1918 Fire

Donn Larson —
Duluth-Superior's
Greatest PR practioner
+ an old friend.

David Helberg
8/18

savage
PRESS

14172 E Carlson Rd. • Brule, WI 54820
(218) 391-3070 • www.savpress.com

Thomson Township's
NIGHT OF TERROR
The Great 1918 Fire

C. PHILIP JOHNSON, RODNEY IKOLA
AND DAVIS HELBERG

First Edition

Editor: Davis Helberg
Writers: C. Philip Johnson, Rodney Ikola, Davis Helberg
Researchers: Connie Jacobson, Julie Kesti
Esko Historical Society President: Ronald Sillanpa
Cover Design and Layout: Dezime Graphics

ISBN: 9781937706203

Library of Congress Catalog Number:

Published by:
    Savage Press
    14172 E Carlson Rd.
    Brule, WI 54820
    Email: mail@savpress.com
    Website: www.savpress.com
    Printed in the United States of America

Preface

ANSWERING SOME QUESTIONS

This book, encouraged and sponsored by the Esko Historical Society, commemorates the centennial of the most significant day in Thomson Township history, a terrible, frightful day that would forever change the township's northern landscape while also becoming the catalyst for creation of a new school district that led to the growth and development of the community that became known as Esko.

Much of the research about October 12, 1918, and the great fire of that day had already been done and was included in a main story of *Esko's Corner, an Illustrated History of Esko and Thomson Township*, published at the end of 2013.

But certain questions remained. How many victims were township residents? How much of the township actually burned? Were there other written or oral memoirs in existence not included in Esko's Corner? Were there more photos?

A half-dozen former and present township residents began to seek answers to these and other questions in the summer of 2017. Davis Helberg, Connie Jacobson, Phil Johnson and Rodney Ikola had all worked on the *Esko's Corner* volume and they were joined by Julie Kesti and Esko Historical Society President Ronald Sillanpa.

Their research and writing—plus the invaluable contributions of those who responded to the call for new information—resulted in this book, *Thomson Township's Night of Terror.*

The historical society and the book committee are grateful to the new contributors as well as to Community Printing, Cloquet; the Duluth Public Library; the Cloquet Public Library; the Carlton County Recorder's Office; the Carlton County Historical Society; the Northeast Minnesota Historical Center, Mike Savage of Savage Press, Superior; layout designer Debra Zime, Barnum; and Bang Printing, Brainerd.

Esko, Minnesota
March 2018

DEDICATION

This book is dedicated to the memories of the men, women and children who lost their lives in the 1918 Fire as well as to those who suffered life-changing injuries. It is also dedicated to those whose homes, barns, cattle and other property were destroyed by the flames. And it is further dedicated to those who, despite losing most or all of their earthly possessions, rose up to help create a new community we now call Esko.

TABLE OF CONTENTS

INTRODUCTION

AN EPIC MOMENT IN A FATEFUL YEAR

C. Philip Johnson

Thick, acrid smoke filled the air in the early evening of October 12, 1918. A northwest wind, rising in intensity, soon carried not just smoke but ash and embers from a giant forest fire which would sweep through the northern half of Thomson Township, burning to death at least 11 people and destroying scores of houses and barns.

A century has passed since that fateful day. Witnesses to the fire are gone now, but many left written memoirs and oral histories so their descendants might understand the events of that one brief moment in 1918.

In 1918 Thomson Township was a land of dairy farms. The men, most of them first- or second- generation Finnish immigrants, had established small, typically 40-acre farms and worked the land with their wives and, usually, a large group of children.

It was still a time of what later was called "stump farming" because many fields were still dotted with enormous white pine stumps, leftovers of the logging era. Farmers simply plowed and planted around the obstacles.

A trip to town involved hitching up the wagon to a single horse or a team. At least Harney, a small community at the junction of Harney and Marks Road and the site of the Duluth, Winnipeg & Pacific Railroad depot, now had a general store, meaning that families no longer had to travel all the way to Ruikka's Store in the small village of Thomson for their staples.

Except for a small school and an intersection that routed traffic from Duluth either south to St. Paul or west toward Cloquet, the community of Esko did not yet exist.

School-age children walked to one-room schoolhouses; 10 of them were scattered throughout the township. Three of the northernmost schools burned in the 1918 Fire, prompting a new school district to reorganize in 1919 and 1920.

1918 also would be remembered for the world-wide Spanish Flu pandemic that took the lives of at least 10,000 Minnesotans. Despite the efforts of the Minnesota Home Guard, which established an influenza hospital in the village of Thomson for all county residents, many who escaped the Cloquet Fire eventually succumbed to the flu.

World War I was nearly over. American soldiers had been bloodied at two battles at France's Chateau-Thierry and Belleau Wood. They now were part of the final assaults on Germany's Hindenburg Line and families like the Seikkulas, Harneys, Perttulas and Niemis worried about their sons serving in the AEF, the American Expeditionary Force.

The war in France and Germany wasn't the only conflict on people's minds. The Russian Revolution of the previous year had spilled over to neighboring Finland, which declared its independence on December 6, 1917. Since so many families had relatives in the "old country," news of the White and Red forces battling in the Finnish Civil War created considerable anxiety.

Any news from Europe came from letters or an occasional newspaper one might buy at the store. Radio had not yet arrived to provide more current information. Some farms had telephones, but lines had just started to appear in 1917 so not everyone could reach their neighbors that way.

No one foresaw the terrifying events of October 12. The firestorm which descended on the township that evening ended the lives of many and, one could argue, changed the lives of all.

This location is unknown but typical of what northern township residents would have witnessed the morning after the fire.
(Photo by Hugh McKenzie, widely known Duluth photographer of that era)

CHAPTER 1

TERROR IN THOMSON TOWNSHIP

C. Philip Johnson

The 1929 stock market crash. Pearl Harbor. The day President Kennedy was shot. 9/11. Traumatic events serve as dividing lines in an individual's life. One's memory is often split into parts as in "before Pearl Harbor" or "after 9/11."

For first- and second-generation Thomson Township immigrants, the event that became their "before and after" was the 1918 Fire.

Described at length in the Esko Historical Society's 2014 book, *Esko's Corner, An Illustrated History of Esko and Thomson Township*, the 1918 Fire (also known as the Cloquet or Cloquet-Moose Lake Fire) remains the deadliest natural disaster in state history. At least 453 people perished—the exact number will never be known—including at least 11 and possibly 13 Thomson Township residents.

The fire, actually made up of over four (some sources claim five) dozen individual blazes, burned 1,500 square miles, nearly twice the size of Carlton County.

In order for a fire of this magnitude to happen, certain natural conditions need to be in place. Lengthy dry spells or drought, an abundance of natural fuel, low humidity, strong winds and a fire source create these conditions. All these factors occurred in October 1918.

First, northern Minnesota was experiencing an extremely dry fall which followed the dry years of 1916 and 1917. Dry leftover wood, called slash, from logging operations provided the fuel. October 12 saw extremely low humidity (registering at 21 percent in Duluth, 19 points below average). Residents noticed winds becoming stronger throughout the day. They measured 60 mph in Duluth and were estimated to be 80 mph in front of the fire.

Multiple ignition sources have been identified by historians, with sparks from railroad steam locomotives being the primary factor. Today, these combined elements would result in a burning ban enforced by the Minnesota Department of Natural Resources. In 1918 there was no such central government oversight.

Although 20 years after the fire, big burnt stumps still remained on some northern
township farmland. Until the stumps were removed, farmers (and cattle)
often worked around them. The photo was taken in about 1940.
(Esko Historical Society photo from 1940-41 FFA scrapbook)

The conflagration in Thomson Township was part of the massive
Cloquet burn which roared eastward, finally ending on the western edge
of present day Proctor and looping around Duluth to the North Shore.
It was said that the only reason Duluth was spared was an east wind off
Lake Superior on October 13.

Numerous personal histories, some written and others oral recordings,
describe the nightmare struggles of October 12. Although each resident
experienced the fateful event in a unique way, there were many common
threads.

The day started out as a beautiful October fall morning. People did
notice smoke in the air, but evidently that was little cause for concern. In
fact, there had been many smoky days that fall. In addition to the logging
companies burning slash, some farmers burned fields after harvest, and
other farmers were still clearing land and burning brush.

So farmwives started their day by baking bread or washing clothes.
The menfolk resumed fall plowing or were engaged in other farm chores.
It was Saturday, meaning the saunas would be fired up in the afternoon.
For many neighbors, gathering for Saturday sauna was a weekly social
event.

Scenes such as this would have been common on area roads the morning after
the fire. The location is unknown, except that information accompanying
the photo indicated it was taken in Carlton County.
(Carlton County Historical Society)

By midafternoon the smoke became thicker, but most township
residents just regarded it as a nuisance. They didn't know, in this era
before rapid communication (most residents did not have telephones),
that fellow Minnesotans 20 miles to the northwest in the Brookston area
were running for their lives. A steam locomotive had sparked a small
blaze two days earlier near Milepost 62, four miles west of Brookston on
the Great Northern Railroad line. The railroad did send out small crews
to try to extinguish the fire, but it blew up out of control on October 12.

By about 4 p.m., news of impending disaster reached Thomson
Township.

Many families sent men to the area north of Cloquet to fight the
oncoming flames. What did they hope to accomplish with minimal
equipment or organization? What motivated them to leave their own
homes? For some it was a desire to help neighbors or relatives save their
farms. Others wanted to stop the fire before it came too close—burning
embers were already appearing miles ahead of the main fire line. Their
efforts, however, proved futile.

By early evening each farm family had to make an excruciating choice—run from the oncoming flames or stay to try and save their homes, barns and livestock. Cedar shingles were common on homes and barns. Some smaller outbuildings may have had birch bark shingles. Unless a farm had a gasoline water pump and hose, all the water would have to be applied by hand via a bucket brigade. If a family received adequate warning, they hand-pumped water and filled every available barrel and container. One or two people climbed onto roofs and pulled water buckets up by hand to douse the flames. After decades of backbreaking work, families were willing to risk their lives to save their farms.

Many others could not or did not place themselves in such great peril. For them, the impending darkness hid their race for survival. In fact the terror of the moment was worsened since such flights took place close to or after sundown, and the thick smoke made the twilight much darker.

A brief description in the *Cloquet Pine Knot* illustrates one nightmarish flight: "C.D. Andrews and wife and Mr. and Mrs. Davis left by car about 10:30 p.m. for safety from the fire. No notable problems arose as they crossed the Scanlon bridge and went east toward Duluth... on the 'old right-of-way' to about one-half mile west of Alex Esko's homestead. There, fire blocked their escape...Mr. Andrews backed the car up...and turned south...on a 'farmer road.' Then he drove east to the Duluth road...but was met by cars heading west since the road was closed at the Canadian Northern trestle...Then Mr. Andrews went to Carlton on the road through the Village of Thomson, both of which were smoky but safe from the tongues of fire elsewhere."

Some who fled found refuge in the middle of plowed fields which created firebreaks.

Others ran south to the Midway River and spent the night in its currents.

Like in neighboring Cloquet, the railroad came to the rescue. Only one railroad, the Duluth Winnipeg and Pacific (DW&P), now the Canadian National, had active operations in the northern part of the township impacted by the fire. It was along the DW&P track that rescue efforts were made.

One DW&P train attempted to travel through the fire from the north. It was stopped by a small burning trestle spanning a small stream just north of the Stark Road, so the train barely made it into the township. As far as is known, that train failed to rescue anyone.

A second DW&P train was mobilized from West Duluth, passed through Harney and proceeded as far as the Stark Road where it was stopped by the same burning bridge. It backed up to Harney, picking up fleeing families along the way as well as a group gathered at or near the depot. Jennie Kinnunen Sota (1897-1981) remembered the train blew its whistle continually throughout its rescue attempt, hoping to guide people in the darkness.

At dawn on October 13 survivors drifted back to their farms or went to check up on neighbors. They had no idea that nearby Cloquet was virtually destroyed. The southern half of Thomson Township was spared (see map), so some found temporary refuge with more fortunate friends or relatives.

But despite the fact that the fire path stayed to the north, the heavy smoke and high winds, along with reports from fleeing residents, would have caused considerable anxiety in the southern part of the township, too. Robert D. Esko wrote the following in *Esko's Corner* regarding the experiences of his community namesake grandparents, whose home was south of the highway above the Midway River:

"Alex and Eva Esko's farmstead was spared, but just barely. A fierce wind whipped glowing embers from burning trees all across the landscape.

"Residents along…the highway spent the night soaking burlap sacks in water, then climbing ladders and laying the wet sacks on the wood shingles of their roofs. Alex and his sons worked hard to protect their buildings and they succeeded, but they were fortunate to be the south edge of the conflagration, so they escaped serious damage."

Mary (Oja) Helberg (1910-1992) was an 8-year-old on her parents' farm on today's Oja Road, south of the highway about a mile east of Scanlon. She remembered the entire family engaged throughout the night in wetting down the house and barn roofs. The buildings were saved—but in a twist of irony, the house burned down the following spring.

Because of the disaster's magnitude, the 1918 fire is one of the most researched events in local history. One of the most complete histories is *The Fires of Autumn* by Francis Carroll and Franklin Raiter, published in 1990 by the Minnesota Historical Society Press. In early 2018, the same publisher released *Minnesota 1918, When Flu, Fire and War Ravaged the State*, by Curt Brown. Many other sources are available at the Carlton County Historical Society.

Despite these records, not much has been recorded heretofore about the experience of Thomson Township residents. This may be due to the extent of the disaster in other areas of Carlton County. The dramatic rescue by trains of 7,000 to 8,000 Cloquet area residents on the evening of October 12 and the large number of fatalities in the Moose Lake/ Kettle River area has understandably drawn the lion's share of interest by historians. But to a Thomson Township resident who lost a farm or, worse yet, a family member or a close neighbor, the tragedy was no less real or overwhelming.

To understand what happened on that Saturday it is best to let the survivors or their children speak for themselves. When the Esko Historical Society embarked on the five-year *Esko's Corner* book project, society members went out with digital recorders to preserve residents' memories. (More recently, a call went forth soliciting additional family memories or newly discovered material, and they have been added to this book.)

The following short narratives, preceded by the names of those interviewed, are from those or other oral records or, as noted, from written articles and memoirs. Longer narratives are set apart in separate chapters and are included later.

*   *   *

Louis Fredrickson (1916-2012):

I was 2 years old at the time of the Cloquet Fire. I remember watching with my folks behind the house to see how close the fire was going to come. It didn't cross the Midway River; the wind was in the right direction. We saw the flames and wondered how close it was going to come. It burned a lot of places north of us. Nothing happened on the south side of Esko. There was nothing left but stumps where it burned. Esko's Corner buildings survived. [11]

Mamie Juntunen Hjulberg (1903-1998):

My generation marks time by "before the fire" and "after the fire"... The folks on the farm first planned to go to Harney and take a train, but when they got to Olson's bridge (Harney Road) they decided to stay by the river...Harneys were the only people in Section 16 whose house didn't burn...

I was in Cloquet working for my board and room while going to high school. My employers decided to load their car and go to Carlton. I helped them load it and fed the baby his bottle. Then they told me there wasn't room for me in the car and I should go to my sisters. As they lived out in the west end (of Cloquet) I had a long walk to 15th street.

I met people on the sidewalk going toward the depot but I expected to get to Johnsons before they left. When I got there everyone was gone. I saw a man who I knew who was in his car. I told him about my predicament. He asked if I had any money and I told him I only had a nickel. He said to go back to the depot and get on a train.

A woman came out of the Crescent Hotel and together we faced the strong winds and the smoke. When we were up to the fire hall a police car picked us up. He had us go under a fence to a box car as the depot was on fire. When we got into the box car I heard a man say the Masonic Temple walls had fallen down. We were taken to Carlton and put on a train to Duluth. The Red Cross was there. They had us single women go to the YWCA...

They took me in the morning to where fire refugees were, but I didn't find anyone I knew. At the depot one woman was telling that she had come on the Canadian Northern Railroad and all of the town of Thomson was on fire and the only people who survived were a small group who took the train from Harney. I said, "That's where my folks live." Another woman put her arm around me and said, "Don't worry, if you lost your family, I'll adopt you."

Sunday night I was able to reach Kate (a sister). She was working in Gary. She had been on the farm and said everyone was safe. Mother said she had such strong faith that we'd all be safe.

Glenn Juntunen (1930-2018):

My parents moved here (to their farm) just two weeks before the fire. Just one little hayshed burned here…That day of the fire Grandpa Juntunen tried to get a potato out of a cow's throat, but the cow died. It burned up in (near) the river. Ashes were flying, but Grandpa went on the roof to put them (out). The wind was so strong that the water came back at him. Pieces of wood were blowing through the air; the wind was blowing so hard! Then the wind shifted another way and saved the place.

"Kayo"(Leslie) Kesti (1930-2013):

My parents Hannes (Hans) Kesti (1888-1972) and Ida Kesti (1888-1968) were on the farm with three kids—seven-year-old John (1911-1966); five-year-old George (1913-1989); and two-year-old Elna (1916-2009)…They were undecided if they should go with the people who were escaping the fire to the railroad crossing or section in the township…Pa decided that they would stay; it probably wasn't the right thing to do, Pa later said. Ma was pumping water and hooking the pail of water on a rope and John was on the roof to get it…They managed to save the house with its wood shingles…They saved the house but lost the buildings…It was quite a decision (to stay) with the fire burning all around and other people leaving with horses and wagons. They stayed and elected to save the house—they could have lost five lives! Pa said it was really sad that fall and there wasn't a single green tree standing. The fire didn't burn all of the trees completely, but killed the trees and left them standing, dead. They had lots of firewood that winter…

Bill Bohren (1903-2003):

On the morning of October 12, 1918, our family awakened to a very smoky and windy day, but it wasn't until the afternoon that we considered the smoke and fire was a very severe matter. Our neighbor's house was on fire. Although we lived in Carlton County, the road that separated us from St. Louis County and the (neighbor's) burning house was easily seen from our yard.

My dad, my brother Fred (1900-1992) and I gathered all the equipment such as shovels, axes and so forth that we could carry, and along with my little dog Spot, we ran all the one-half or three-quarters of a mile up the road to the neighbor's house…to help them.

That being accomplished, we turned our attention homeward, for sparks were flying all over the place and before we had gone far we faced a wall of fire about 30 feet wide. This is where Spot chose not to stay the course and turned back. We could not find him, due to the heavy smoke and fire. Thus, with a heavy heart, I continued on to my home to do what I had to do to help save our own farm.

Fortunately we had a good well, with a little gasoline engine that could and did pump enough water for the five of us—my mother, sister Ida (1901-1999), my dad, brother Fred and myself—to save our farm. All we lost was one little hay shed and my dog.

It was midnight before we dared stop hauling water and by that time, having a history of migraine headaches, I was ready to collapse, which I did. After taking several aspirins, I fell into bed and the next morning at five o'clock I was able to get up and help milk our 28 cows, which had not been milked the night before.

All in all, this was the worst day so far, of my ninety-five-year life.

Vieno Savo (1909-1998), memories as submitted by daughter Verna (Pantsar) Flynn:

We attended the Huot School, a two-mile hike from our home. During the fall we shortened the distance by a mile by taking a short cut through the woods. The school was a bit larger than the average country school—it had three classrooms. In the winter when the snow was too deep, we could not use the shorter route. Instead we mounted the drifts and marched to school. The drifts were (sometimes) so high we could touch the telephone wires from pole to pole.

I was nine years old when the Huot School fell victim to the 1918 forest fire. The fire also attacked the Savo farm on October 12. My mother pumped water from the well while the older children formed a bucket brigade to our father and uncle who would throw water on the blaze until it finally was extinguished. The fire was contained to one end of the house so it wasn't difficult to repair the damage. One week later, on October 19, another baby was born to the Savo family.

People who were not so fortunate as us walked past our farm in search of a place to stay. Some stopped to see if there was room in our house. My mother and dad took in as many as they could. By the end of the week, 24 people were crammed into our home.

We children went to school now being held in the Thomson Town Hall. It was the school from 1918 until 1920 when the Washington School was built...and the displaced students had a new hall of learning. I was 14 when I graduated from Washington's eighth grade.

John ("Ivar") Heini, *from a memoir submitted by granddaughter Virginia (Heini) Hatinen, also the granddaughter of Carl ("Sam") Hatinen*:

My grandfather came to the U.S. from Finland and found employment as a teamster among the Cloquet lumber and paper mill. His name was John "Ivar" Heini (pronounced hay-knee).

He and his team of horses made numerous trips out of the surrounding areas and were instrumental in transporting many evacuees to the train depot. The loaded trains took the people to Duluth.

Unfortunately for my family, after the last train left Cloquet, my grandfather was unable to save his team of horses from the fire. This major loss took a heavy toll on him and caused him significant health issues. He became hospitalized at the state hospital in Willmar. He remained hospitalized for several years and died at a young age.

He died long before I was born so I was never able to meet him. He is buried in Willmar.

Carl S. ("Sam") Hatinen (1919-1995), *submitted by his son, Ray S. Hatinen*:

The Hatinen family was in the process of developing a farm on the Hatinen Road. The family (Waino and Eva and sons Waino and Samuel) had cleared areas for gardening, farm crops, and pasture. As time permitted, they were clearing additional areas for farming.

In October 1918, Eva was expecting and was about six months into the pregnancy. On October 12, the fire hazard was increasing dramatically to the point where the family needed to flee to save their lives. The Juntunen family had a farm to the east that had larger clearings to provide a buffer from the flames. A fork of Crystal Creek separated the two farms.

Abel took son Waino while Eva took two-year-old Samuel and tried to outrun the fast approaching flames. Eva was short (maybe 4-foot-10) and heavy with her six-month pregnancy. She couldn't keep up with the others and found that the only option would be to seek refuge in the creek. Even though the fall was very dry, there was water in the creek, but not enough to immerse themselves. As a result, Eva and Samuel were badly burned as the fire swept over them.

Eva and Samuel were transported to a Duluth hospital and began treatment for their burns. Young Samuel lived about two days but did not survive his injuries...Eva was hospitalized for an extended period but did survive. Her pregnancy continued during the recovery and she delivered another boy, Carl Sam Hatinen—who went by Sam his whole life—on January 25, 1919 in their sauna.

Abe and Eva were both emigrants from Finland and did not understand much of the English language. Their thinking was that since Samuel had died as a result of the fire, they could not give the newborn son the same name.

So my dad became Carl Samuel Hatinen, [but] the family disregarded the official name and called my dad "Sammy" or "Sam" for his entire life. My dad found out his official name when he entered the Army during WW II. He was asked to show his birth certificate. When he saw his birth certificate for the first time, he didn't believe it was his and asked his parents, "Who is this Carl?" My dad continued to use the name "Sam C." Hatinen for the remainder of his life.

EXTENT OF 1918 FIRE
THOMSON TOWNSHIP

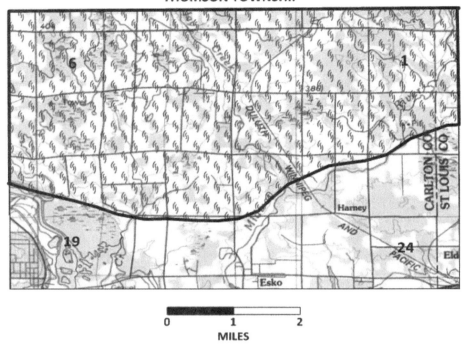

Map by Rodney Ikola.

RECONSTRUCTIION OF THE FIRE PATH

Rodney Ikola

In the aftermath of the fires, two public agencies produced maps showing the extent of the burned areas: Minnesota Forest Service (MFS) and Governor's Fire Relief Commission (GFRC). Both maps generally agree on the broad outlines of the fires but diverge on the details.

In Thomson Township both maps show the fire going as far south as modern-day Esko, with the GFRC map further suggesting a lobe of the fire extended an additional mile and a half to the south. Both maps also show the fire extending at least one mile south of Harney.

Numerous family histories and oral interviews collected by the Esko Historical Society suggest both maps are incorrect in depicting the southern edge of the fire. Eyewitness recollections from individuals living a half-mile north of Esko describe seeing the fire burning to the north of their residence. Individuals displaced by the fire were temporarily housed at farms not destroyed between Harney and Midway River.

This map shows the southern edge of the fire as best reconstructed from these personal observations. The fire extended to the northern edge of the township and for many miles beyond. Only at the extreme western and eastern margins of the map is the south edge of the fire in doubt; eyewitness accounts are sparse or lacking in those areas.

Part of the problem in depicting the extent of the fire is undoubtedly due to the erratic nature of the burned areas. For example, Nopeming Sanatorium, one mile east of the southeast corner of the map, was evacuated due to isolated fires burning in the vicinity. Within the fire area, numerous structures were not destroyed because the fire jumped over them. Early newspaper accounts may also have contributed to the inaccuracy of the early maps. Harney and the surrounding area were erroneously reported to have been engulfed in flames in some of the early stories.

Chapter 2

Confirmed Victims; Were There More?

Rodney Ikola

Following is a list of confirmed fire victims in Thomson Township as well as certain information regarding their origins and places of residence. The final death toll will never be known for certain because some township victims may have died days or weeks later in Duluth or Superior or some other area and their deaths may have been recorded elsewhere. Additionally, Spanish flu, raging through the nation, may also have claimed persons who survived the fire but whose weakened conditions left them vulnerable to the flu.

*   *   *

Jennie Swanson.   She lived with her brother Albert Swanson who owned a 40-acre farm at the northeast corner of the Ikola and Stark Roads. She was born in Sweden on Jan. 23, 1861, and was single, living with her brother at the time of her death on Oct. 12, 1918. According to death records, she was a housewife with cause of death (COD) listed as "burned by forest fire."

Maria Nasi.   She and her husband Andrew (he is listed as John in the 1910 Federal census) owned a 40-acre farm along the east side of Church Ave. a half mile north of the North Cloquet Road. She was born June 21, 1850, in Finland and succumbed to burns in the forest fire on Oct. 12, 1918. According to death records, COD is listed as "burned in forest fire." Selma Ikola recalled she "burned by the side of the road."

Josephine Uponen.   She and her husband John owned a 40-acre farm a quarter-mile north of the Stark Road which was crossed by the Duluth Winnipeg & Pacific Railroad. She was born in Finland in July 1868 and succumbed to effects from the fire on Oct. 12, 1918. Death records list COD as "suffocation and burns in forest fire." The tragedy of the Uponen family was magnified by the actions of the husband on the day of the fire. With the arrival of the fire storm imminent, he ordered his wife and three children to stay home while he sought the safety of a neighbor's home. The next morning his wife was found burned on the ground, the burned bodies of two girls in one washtub and the burned body of the boy in another washtub. Evidently the mother had tried to save her children by immersing them in water filled washtubs. To add insult to the tragedy, the husband, who was a township constable, was allegedly seen mourning over the fact that all his paper money had burned.

Martha Elizabeth Uponen. Daughter of Josephine and John Uponen. Born July 11, 1906, and succumbed to the fire on Oct. 12, 1918. COD listed as "suffocation and burns in forest fire."

Mary Elnore Uponen. Daughter of Josephine and John Uponen. Born January 9, 1907, and succumbed to fire on Oct. 12, 1918. COD listed as "suffocation and burns in forest fire."

John William Uponen. Son of Josephine and John Uponen. Born April 14, 1914, and succumbed to fire on Oct. 12, 1918. COD listed as "suffocation and burns in forest fire."

Sophia Puotinen. Wife of Pastor Alex Puotinen, she and her husband owned a 40-acre farm on the northwest corner of Harney and Canosia Roads. She was born in Finland in 1854 and succumbed to the fire on Oct. 14, 1918. COD listed as "suffocation by smoke." Some difficulty was experienced in locating this name in the county records because it is listed as Pnotinen.

Sandra Mickelson. She and her husband John owned a 40-acre farm on the southwest corner of North Cloquet and Himango Roads. She was born in Finland in 1884 and succumbed to the fire on Oct. 12, 1918. COD listed as "burned in forest fire." Some documents list the family name as Michaelson.

Helen Maria Mickelson. Daughter of Sandra and John Mickelson, she was born December 25, 1908, and succumbed to the fire on Oct. 12, 1918. COD listed as "burned in forest fire." Some documents list her name as Helli.

Samuel Henry Hatinen. Son of Eva and Abel Hatinen who had property along the Hatinen Road. He was born on April 14, 1916, and died Oct. 22, 1918, from injuries suffered in the forest fire. On the day of the fire the Hatinen family fled their farm, attempting to get to the Joseph Juntunen farm for safety. Eva, who was pregnant, and young Sam could not run fast enough and sought shelter in Crystal Creek. However, the water was not deep enough to submerge them and they were partially burned by the fire. Transported to a Duluth hospital, Samuel eventually succumbed to his injuries.

Theodore Erwin Barney. Son of Edwin and Jennie Barney, he was born June 14, 1917, and succumbed to injuries sustained during the fire on Oct. 12, 1918. COD is recorded as "skull fractured by auto while escaping forest fire."

(Note: Could the mother have been Jennie Forstie Barney even though the county records say Jennie *Foostie* Barney? Jennie Forstie Barney was born Dec. 10, 1896, to Matt and Sophia Forstie, longtime Thomson Township residents, and died Jan. 25, 1919, due to tuberculosis and is listed as a widow. There is a Jennie Forstie Barney buried at the Apostolic Lutheran Cemetery in Esko. There is no Edwin Barney in the records, but there is an Edward Paarni, born in Finland on Feb. 22, 1892, and died August 31, 1917. His parents were Joseph and Christina Paarni who were not the parents of longtime resident George Barney (Paarni); possibly Joseph and George's father were brothers? If the above speculation is correct, Theodore's father died when Theodore was only 2 ½ months old and why Jennie is listed as a widow in her death certificate.)

An accurate list of deaths is hard to establish. For example, some oral and written memoirs mention a "baby Mickelson" and a Mrs. Maki. A search of county death records, however, revealed no such individuals.

A Duluth News Tribune reporter, traveling by train to the fire area on October 13, described seeing 11 bodies in Harney (probably lined up near the depot.) This wasn't the only makeshift morgue. A barn still standing on the Donald A. Pykkonen farm was used as a temporary morgue (see Chapter 10).

Newspapers also listed dead and injured in editions within a week.

These lists are inaccurate. For example, some known township residents are listed as Cloquet residents. Many victims are described as living on North Road, the present North Cloquet Road. Were these victims in the township or not? Another rather vague address is "Route 1 Cloquet." Rural residents of the township were part of the Cloquet Post Office's Route 1 until the mid-1960s. Some injured victims made it to Duluth hospitals, only to succumb from their injuries later on. They certainly were fire deaths, but are listed in St. Louis County, not Carlton County, records.

And families like Nik and Riika Johnson would suffer emotionally. The Johnsons lived just west of the Harney bridge on the Marks Road. Because of the horrific fire sweeping in from the west, Riika delivered a stillborn baby on October 12. She kept the baby with her in bed throughout the night. One can only imagine what she heard and thought during those long dark hours.

In the wake of the fire, area residents faced massive rebuilding projects, but some things—like these giant trees uprooted by the gale force winds—could not be reconstructed. *(Photo from "The Fury of the Flames," published in 1919)*

CHAPTER 3

'WORLD FULL OF SMOKE'

Davis Helberg

On September 27, 1918, Charles A. Nelson's daily journal included the following: "Cloudless, very smoky, fires somewhere."

On the following day, Nelson wrote: "Getting dryer & dryer every day."

A few days later in his monthly summary, he wrote, "A rather warm September, but very dry, too dry, forest-fire making."

It was a prophetic observation, as we now know, and similar entries would be made through October 12, the day of the fire, and beyond.

At the time, Nelson, born in 1889, was farming with his father, Henry Nelson (originally Heikki Laakso), in Section 9 west of Canosia Road. Charles inherited the farm after his father's death in 1924.

A community leader for decades, Nelson served among other things as school board treasurer, insurance

Charles A. Nelson was 29 at the time of the fire. The year of this photo is not known, but Nelson appears to be in his late 20s or early 30s. *(Photo courtesy of Jody Acers, Cloquet)*

company treasurer, telephone company auditor, township election clerk, Finnish interpreter and legal aide.

He also was a dedicated journal keeper nearly all of his adult life, writing every day about the weather, farm work, family matters, visits with neighbors and general observations about community life. Following are selected excerpts of his October 1918 diaries:

Oct. 1: "Very strong west [winds]. Clear, too dry, forest fires raging."

Oct. 2: "Brisk NW [winds]. Clear and dry and smoky."

Oct. 9: "70 [high temperature}. Brisk NW. Clear and pleasant."

Oct. 10: "72. Brisk west. Clear. Very pleasant and warm."

Oct. 11: "Mostly cloudy, smoky."

Oct. 12: "74. Very fierce NW. Cloudless, world full of smoke. Fighting fires p.m. Fire swept over settlement, burning houses and killing people. Our loss: 3 hay sheds."

> *Later, Nelson would describe the fire like this: "Everyone who went through the fire will forever remember the horrible experiences, the roaring, rolling flames, the fearful wind, the smoke and dust and flying embers, the difficulty breathing and the straining of the last atom of strength in fighting the fire."*

Following October 12, Nelson continued to make periodic references to fires, to wit:

Oct. 13: "Brisk west. Cloudless, but smoky. Fighting fires a.m. Was taken to Proctor hospital p.m. to receive treatment for burned eyes."

Oct. 14: "Came home from Proctor p.m. The country is laid desolate and devastated by the fire."

Oct. 15: "Fighting the fires. Strenuous times."

Oct. 20: "Fighting and watching the fires most of the day."

Oct. 21: "Watching fires."

Oct. 22: "Clear dry, too dry. Watching the fires most of the day."

Then, finally, the threat apparently ended:

Oct. 25: "Cloudy, snowing p.m."

Oct. 26: "Light rain and snow."

In his October summary, Nelson wrote: "Memorable forever for its fearful forest fires in which N.E. Minnesota was burned up. Spanish flu also started its ravages."

Beginning Oct. 31, and continuing well into the 1930s, the diaries routinely refer to his work as a local insurance company official as he and his colleagues assessed property damage, wrote reports, paid claims, met with attorneys, conducted meetings, etc.

Given the devastation of the 1918 Fire, fall weather-watching took on greater significance for years to come, including these increasingly anxious references two years later, in October 1920:

Oct. 8: "Smoke from big forest fire in Wisconsin can be seen."

Oct. 9: "Forest fire menace growing."

Oct. 10: "Fire menace growing grave."

Oct. 11: "People anxiously waiting for rain."

Oct. 12: "Still no rain. Dry, dry, too dry."

Oct. 13: "Very heavy and destructive thunderstorm and rain. Forest fire menace surely at an end now. Lightning did some damage in neighborhood."

Oct. 14: "People feeling relieved because no danger of fires anymore."

Among the final references to the Fire are these in his annual summary of 1935: "The 1918 Fire Claims were passed by Congress. There is hope of getting the money." And at the end of 1936: "The government 1918 fire money enabled us to pay off the mortgage on our land."

*   *   *

The Esko Historical Society is grateful to Cloquet's Jody Acers and her mother, Anita (Nelson) Anderson, a 1947 Esko graduate, for preserving and sharing their grandfather's/father's priceless insights into several decades of local history. Within the family, Charles Nelson is still remembered as "humble, kind" and a lover of animals who also "admired poetry, music and art." He farmed and maintained his diaries until the late 1950s. He died on August 18, 1960.

CHAPTER 4

A LASTING MEMORIAL

Davis Helberg

Until the fall of 2017, the great 1918 Fire was remembered in Thomson Township mainly by the stories of the survivors, stories that were passed along from one generation to the next.

But stories are fragile things, embellished by some, forgotten by others.

Now, however, there's also a memorial monument, one that should endure for a long time, unchanging, as permanent as stone.

Carved from black granite, polished to a high gleam, it's nearly eight feet tall, five feet wide, and it stands in the cemetery of St. Matthews Lutheran Church at the intersection of North Cloquet Road and Church Avenue.

The St. Matthews church of today is just off Highway 61 near Esko's town center, but from 1903 to 1961 it was on the west side of the cemetery, part of a four-acre site donated by nearby farmer Kalle Pykkonen.

Prior to the fire, the names of those buried in the cemetery were inscribed on wooden grave markers. But although the church survived, the grave markers were all destroyed—as were records of their locations because they were kept at homes that also burned.

"The area of those first gravesites was passed down from generation to generation, so we knew where they were," said Don W. Pykkonen, who led the effort to construct a monument. "But we were concerned the information could be lost in the future.

"We're not getting any younger, so we decided in 2015 that we've got to do this [create a permanent monument] now."

Pykkonen, a retired banker whose grandfather, Matt, was a distant relative of Kalle Pykkonen, assembled an ad hoc committee. Longtime cemetery manager Gene Lindquist, a retired Carlton County road supervisor, became the committee's co-chair.

Duluth Monument Company manager Leo Koski, whose grandmother was raised in the township, gave Pykkonen and Lindquist the idea for black granite. It's not produced in the United States, however, so a block of it was imported from India. The carving and inscriptions were done by a company in Little Falls, Minnesota.

The finished product was erected in September 2017 in the northwest part of the cemetery without public attention because an official dedication was set for October 12, 2018. Besides the monument, there are four black granite corner posts outlining the boundaries of the original grave sites, an area of roughly 30 by 45 feet.

On the front of the monument is a finely etched image of the old church, replete with a woman in a long dress sitting on the front steps. Under the image, the inscription reads:

"In memory of those buried in unmarked graves in St. Matthews Lutheran Cemetery from 1903-1918."

On the back, or north side, it reads:

"Dedicated to the memory of those persons buried in the unmarked graves on this site between the years 1903-1918. Official documents of these buried here were kept in homes of church members and most were burned in the massive forest fire of Oct. 12, 1918. The wooden markers or crosses were also burned, leaving these graves unmarked. Early records for the burials of this period have come mostly from memory.

"The original church was situated on the west side of the cemetery and was not destroyed even though the fire came within six inches of the church building."

The wording was drafted by Pykkonen and Lindquist and edited by Phyllis Bohren, a retired Esko teacher and longtime church member.

Total project cost was about $10,000. The money came from two donor-generated sources, the church's memorial fund and its cemetery fund.

St. Matthews Lutheran Church erected this black granite monument as a memorial to members whose wooden grave markers were razed by the 1918 Fire. The monument was to be formally dedicated on October 12, 2018. *(Photo by Davis Helberg)*

CHAPTER 5

FIRE TOOK HEAVY TOLL AMONG ETHNIC FINNS

*Marlene Wisuri, author, artist and publisher (Dovetailed
Press LLC), was director of the Carlton County Historical
Society from 1992 to 2006. She chairs the Sami Cultural
Center of North America board and resides in Duluth.*

The tragic fire story of Thomson Township's Hatinen family, as
related by a grandson [Ray] in the WDSE-TV documentary, *Fires of
1918*, can be seen as symbolic of the suffering of Finnish immigrants
and their families in the fires. A pregnant Eva Hatinen and her two-year-
old son Samuel were badly burned attempting to flee the fire. Little Sam
died in a Duluth hospital 10 days later.

By 1918, many Finnish immigrants had settled in Carlton, St. Louis
and Aitkin counties and had established homes in the City of Cloquet,
villages such as Esko, Kettle River, Cromwell, Automba and Brookston,
and in rural areas scattered throughout the area. They were working in
the mills and woods, farming, and raising families of American-born
children. In 1910, Carlton County was home to 2,785 Finnish people
out of a total population of 17,559, the second largest ethnic group in the
county. Thomson Township, settled by Finnish immigrants, had a large
proportion of ethnic Finnish residents in that era.

The perfect storm that resulted in the fires of October 12, 1918, killed
people and animals, destroyed livelihoods and took scores of schools,
churches, houses and barns, many of them the dovetailed log buildings
of the first generation of immigrants. As the fires swept the region, Finns
were impacted in large and disproportionate numbers.

When the smoke cleared, it was determined that more than 160 ethnic
Finnish people had lost their lives in the fires—or about 35% of the 453
fire fatalities. Of the 11 known fatalities in Thomson Township, 10 had
Finnish backgrounds.

In other parts of Carlton County, entire Finnish families were wiped
out in heartbreaking stories. These included Nick and Hulda Koivisto
who lost seven of their children when they suffocated in a root cellar
where 16 people, including Mrs. Ida Niemi and five of her children

along with Mrs. Clara Berkio and two of her children, died while crowded in with stored potatoes. Nick and Hulda and John Niemi had remained outside the root cellar to pour water on the top and door, only to be horrified to learn everyone inside had perished for lack of oxygen.

The worst influenza epidemic in history also struck in 1918. Fire survivors, weakened by their ordeal in the fires, succumbed to the flu in large numbers. Thomson Township residents Lila and Saima Anttila, who were badly burned and hospitalized for five months, were finally released from the hospital in the spring of 1919 to find they no longer had a home and both their mother and brother George had died of influenza. Saima later wrote, "It was very sad to go home...no mother, no toys, nothing was the same. Father had to be both a mother and a father."

The Finns, exhibiting their characteristic *sisu,* rebuilt their houses, barns and community schools. Thomson Township emerged from the fires with renewed spirit and went on to establish a community of strong schools and the thriving dairy industry it became famous for.

CHAPTER 6

'THE RIVER WAS A REFUGE'

Arvid Konu (1916-2012). Arvid was not quite three years old at the time of the fire. A gifted storyteller, he wrote this in about 2010.

In 1918, the settlers were to face the most serious test of determination and faith. No rain had fallen to nourish the crops and by that fall the earth was totally parched. The area forests were tinder dry and acrid smoke had hung in the air for weeks.

On October 12 the area exploded into an inferno. In a matter of hours the fire swept through the community, devouring what was in its path, burning total farmsteads in some cases, while in others burning one building while sparing another close to it. There was no way to stop the fire.

The Midway River became the escape from fiery death for the Konu family, as well as their cattle, which followed the family into the river and spent the night there with them, in the river. The river was a refuge that saved many of the families in the area.

All the clothing, bedding, sheets, pillows and other keepsakes had been hastily buried in a small gravel pit behind the house to try to save them from the fire. The morning after the fire, at daylight, Dad went to see what had burned during the night. All of the buildings, including the new hip-roof barn, were gone. Miraculously the frame house had been spared. The fire had found the clothes buried in the gravel pit, and they all burned.

A temporary shed was constructed to house the cattle and horse for the winter. Amazingly enough, in all this adversity and loss, it never occurred to them to give up. This was their home! By 1920 a new hip-roof barn was constructed on the same foundation. It still stands today as a monument of the determination of those early settlers...A new stable for two horses was built and it also was large enough to house young livestock.

Saturday night was sauna night. Many of the neighbors came to bathe every Saturday night. This was a joyous event when the children of all ages came together for a night of playing and enjoying a sauna.

Looking back now, night was never so dark for the Konus that the dawn of a new day didn't inspire a new dedication of purpose. Not wind, snow, rain or a variety of pestilences, yea, even fire, could alter the goal that Matti (1864-1947), Laura (1876-1962), and their children had set, with the blessings that God had started. Truly there have been many roses amid the thorns.

This could be the story of many of the pioneers who survived and built a community, its schools and churches. They set the example for generations of people who followed the early settlers. The Finns call it *sisu*. Maybe someone else might have a different name for it. It has been my great pleasure to jot down some of these historic facts as told to me by my parents.

Township residents were well aware of the approaching fire. Many farms sent one man to the area northwest of Cloquet in an attempt to stop the fire at the St. Louis River. However, the wind picked up burning lumber from all the Cloquet mills and the fire spread eastward. Everyone was told to run back home and save their own buildings. This was the first cooperative effort in firefighting in the township.

I was three years old, but I still remember Nels Johnson (1861-1945) carrying me into our farmhouse the morning after the fire. The house was full of exhausted men sleeping on the floor.

Peat deposits throughout the township burned for months afterward. Once the peat burned, the holes would fill with water so there were many potholes scattered throughout the township.

Farming didn't really progress until after the fire. The fire opened Thomson Township into a farming community. As the trees were burned out, the woods were of no value so they cut the trees down that could be sawed into lumber. They built houses and barns out of that lumber…

It's interesting to note that one disaster would open up a community to a prosperous new farming community. As that happened, better barns were built and the herds grew. In 1923 it had progressed to the point where my Dad bought a 1923 Touring Car and started peddling his milk and butter.

The 1918 Fire and the end of WWI with its dynamite opened up the land. It left a lot of wasteland—dead, burned-out forest with nothing. Nobody had the equipment to get rid of those big old pine stumps. DuPont donated their left-over dynamite—thousands of tons—to the farmers. My father went down to Duluth with his horse and wagon, and got a wagon full of dynamite, a row of fuses, and caps. This was a new avenue of prosperity.

When World War I broke out, the railroads were taken over by the government. That included these local railroads—government operated. They were kind of like leased out to the government. At that time they needed all the transportation they could possibly get for the war effort so they had to mobilize all of these engines, cars and tracks. [But] the government was lax at running the railroads.

There were fires all over the place. The trains had open style wheel bearings with wick and oil that could easily catch fire and start fires in the grass besides the railroads. They were constantly fighting fires, and the railroad didn't bother to do anything at all. They just thought that they were cleaning out the area. Well, one day it got away!

The Matt Konu family home, right rear, was spared by the fire but all the other structures in this pre-1918 photo were destroyed. The house still stands near the southeast corner of the North Cloquet-Erickson Road intersection.
(Esko Historical Society photo)

CHAPTER 7

OLD DOG NAMED DOC MAY HAVE SAVED THE DAY

Catherine (Harney) Osbolt (1905-1993). She was 13 in 1918 and lived on a farm on the northeast corner of the Himango-Harney Road intersection. A member of Thomson Township's second class of high school graduates in 1922, Catherine joined the faculty as teacher and coach in about 1930 and taught until the mid-1940s. She wrote these impressions in 1970. They were conveyed to the historical society in 2017 by her niece, Margaret Harney Pagano of Hudson, Florida.

On Saturday, October 12, 1918, at about noon, the sun looked a little strange. At lunch time, Pa and Ma said that there was a fire somewhere in the area to cause the sun to look like that, but we youngsters paid little attention to that, for it seemed to have no connection with us.

Ma wanted to go to Cloquet (about three miles from our farm) that afternoon, as Aunt Ella and Uncle Malachi had sent us a barrel of apples from Wisconsin that needed to be picked up at the depot. Ma also wanted to go to church. James, who was waiting for his eighteenth birthday so that he could go into the Army, drove her to town.

Catherine Harney
(Photo from 1944 Esko yearbook, "The Lincoln Log.")

While they were gone, the sun and sky looked more awesome as the afternoon progressed and my kid brother Martin and I grew uneasy. While we were alone at the house, Pa and my brother Leo and one of the neighbor kids had gone down into the fields to put out a small fire that was smoldering there. The wind was strong that afternoon and fanned up an additional blaze.

We were much relieved when everyone returned to the house. Ma and James returned from town but they told us that when they were at the depot they learned that Brookston was on fire. I knew that Brookston was on the other side of Cloquet so that didn't cause any worry.

Pa and Ma went to milk the cows according to regular routine and then came in for supper. Pa announced that he and the boys would go down and take a look at the fire that they were sure they had put out that afternoon, lest the strong wind might fan it into flame. Ma and I were doing the dishes and cleaning up when there was a knock on our door and a cry of "Mrs. Harney, let us in. Our house is on fire!"

It was our Finn neighbors, Martha Karjala and her mother and younger brother, who lived on the adjoining farm on the north side. They were carrying a few personal belongings in a blanket. This was the first we realized that the fires were nearby. We tried to console Mrs. Karjala who didn't speak a word of English, but she made it plain through Martha that she wanted one of our boys to go and get their brand-new Oakland car out of the barn. Her husband was away in the woods, logging for the winter, and there was no one at home who could drive the car.

The Harney boys were in the fields with Pa. We went outside but the smoke was so thick you couldn't see a thing. We became alarmed because the Harney men were not at home yet. Karjalas wanted us to join them and walk to some open field to safety but Ma would have none of that. Soon Pa and the boys came to report that they had no trouble with the fire in the field. It was out but they reported choking smoke and ashes in their eyes on their return trip to the house—actually getting lost on their own farm from time to time.

While we were excitedly watching the sky and begging the Karjalas not to attempt going on foot, suddenly the sky lit up and we could see their barn totally in flames. That was where the car had been. Their house had already burned. Mrs. Karjala and her kids were frightened and crying but decided to leave for open ground without us.

In the meantime, Pa and the boys had gone to the area around the barn and other buildings, trying to wet them down with pails of water from the well. A big tamarack stump near the road, very close to our driveway, caught fire and was sending out a volley of sparks. Everything was tinder dry since we hadn't had rain for weeks. The leaves were off the willow trees that formed a windbreak to our driveway and had collected there. We knew if they caught fire our house would be burned for sure so we carried water to wet the house down. We all had jobs to do. The boys dug ditches to keep the fire back. Excitement was at fever pitch. When the well went dry it was more disastrous than ever.

I didn't stay outside very long at a time [because] the smoke was so thick and it was unbearably hot. Rolls of fire shot through the air. Much of it was burning hay from the hay sheds that most of the Finnish neighboring farmers had in their fields.

One could also see burning boards and tree branches, all afire, and being tossed about like matches. The wind was wild and hot!

When the well went dry Pa wanted us all to get into the car so that we could leave. Ma urged him to wait as she hurried about. She gathered up important papers from the bookcase drawers in the front room and she sent me scurrying after clothes upstairs. That was a quick trip and I often wonder what I did pick out to take because I was scared to death.

Ma and the boys buried the box of papers in the garden. We loaded up the car, but Ma was very much opposed to leaving the house for the question was where to go? Where was safety? Weren't we safer at home than on the road? We couldn't see!

Finally Pa persuaded Ma to leave. She and I and Martin got into the car. Then James and Leo decided that we couldn't go off and leave our good old faithful dog, Doc, so they went to get him. He was nowhere to be found. After a lot of calling and whistling the boys remembered his favorite haunt whenever he was frightened so they found him under Ma and Pa's bed. It took some time to get him out to the car for he would not budge and finally they resorted to carrying him, in spite of his struggling.

Just when Doc was being lifted into the car, he broke loose again and made a beeline for his doghouse, a place he rarely ever went. Again the boys were in hot pursuit and it took quite a bit of time to forcibly evict him since the doghouse door was so small. In the meantime, the tamarack stump again burst into flames and was shooting sparks, so Pa and Ma left the car and were trying to beat out the flames.

Finally all of us, plus Doc, were in the car. We started for the road. When we got there, the question was which way to turn. There was fire everywhere. Just about this time, the wind seemed to die down a little. Ma and Pa shouted that the wind was shifting its direction. It seemed that some of the smoke had blown away and it was much easier to breathe. In a few minutes, for the first time, we thought our house might not burn. Suddenly the whole sky lit up and our neighbor Kotka's house was on fire. It seemed to be consumed in about five minutes. This was about 10:30 p.m. Karjala's house, which was across the road from Kotka's and much closer to the woods, had burned about seven o'clock. The fire played many freakish pranks, burning some houses and skipping others. It was fiendish!

Our house didn't burn! Perhaps it was because of the delay of trying to save old Doc; actually he saved us and kept us at home where we could fight the fire. The delay was just what was needed. Our firefighting put out the fires near our house. The roads were filled with stalled cars or empty wagons—people had to abandon them. Some were not so fortunate and burned with their vehicles.

I remember that after the wind had subsided, we kids were sent to bed but there wasn't much sleeping done that night. We couldn't wash—no water. The next morning we found some water had run into the well and after repeated washings our faces were almost clean, although the water was full of soot and ashes. When Ma and I combed our hair it broke off in short pieces, a bit singed. The effect on the boys' short hair was less noticeable. When we were as clean as we could get, we all piled into the car to go to church in Cloquet. We got as far as the main road when we met one of our neighbors who told us we couldn't get to church in Cloquet because the city had burned about eight o'clock the evening before.

Karjalas came back the next day. They had run down the road for several miles and had spent the night in a field. They said it was awful. They lived with us for about six weeks until they got a place of their own. We managed nicely in spite of the language barrier with Mrs. Karjala.

The Red Cross did a great deal to provide food and clothing for the victims. I often went with Martha and her mother when they went to the Red Cross headquarters at the Finn Church on the North Road.

Because much of the city of Cloquet had burned, I, a freshman at Cloquet High School, didn't have any place to go to school. After a six-weeks period, the school sessions began in the Garfield School, which was spared in the fire.

Classes were held from 8 a.m. until noon and then the grade school youngsters came in the afternoon. That meant I had to leave home at 6:30 a.m. in order to get to school on time. It was dark and cold on those wintry mornings and occasionally I would get scared by something in the woods—on those mornings I made better time.

To make up for the delayed start to the school year, we had to go to school on Saturdays. I knew that route well and I loved the mornings when Mr. Pollard would pick me up near the paper mill in his fine horse-drawn cutter, complete with fur robe and jingling sleigh bells.

When it came time to rebuild the Thomson Township educational system, there was quite a bit of squabbling about the kind of schools to be built. Pa was an advocate of good schools. He and a few other leaders worked long and hard to get the district to consolidate its schools. The result was the construction of the Lincoln and Washington Schools.

I became a teacher in the Esko school system and in later years I worked for the Red Cross.

CHAPTER 8

5 NEARBY FARMS, GONE OVERNIGHT

Rodney Ikola

Heikki (Henry) Pera (1846-1937) and Johanna Kustaava (Muotka) Pera (1861-1916) emigrated from Muonio, Finland, in 1892 or 1893; the records are unclear on the exact date.

They originally settled in West Duluth, where Henry erected a home on 66th Avenue West from logs he cut on the hillside. At the time the streets were poorly delineated and the house was partially located on the street right-of-way; it was later moved farther onto the Pera property. John, one of the Pera siblings, was born before the house was moved, and he would often tell visitors he was "born in the middle of the street." Along with many other Finns, Henry worked at the coal docks on the waterfront.

In 1896 Henry purchased 40 acres in Thomson Township on the Marks Road from the St. Paul and Duluth Railroad Co. for $200.

Henry traveled on weekends from West Duluth to his newly purchased township property to construct buildings from logs he cut on the property. When construction was nearly completed, Henry, Kustaava and the five children born in West Duluth (Hilda, Oscar, John, Mary and Esther) moved to the township. They stayed for a while at the neighboring Nels Tweith farm until the Pera house was completed.

After the Pera family settled into their new home, four additional children were born (Hilma, Selma, Carl and Elsie). Young Esther died of unknown causes when only a few years old. An even more tragic event occurred in May 1916 when Kustaava succumbed to pneumonia. This left Henry with four young children to raise. A neighbor lady, Caroline Perttula, was instrumental in helping Henry cope with the situation.

By the fall of 1918 a persistent drought was continuing in the northern Minnesota woodlands. Humidity was extremely low, dropping to 21 percent on October 12. Winds started to increase in the afternoon, reaching 30 to 40 miles per hour and then, by early evening, up to 60 miles per hour. It has been estimated the winds were 80 to 90 miles per hour along the fire front. All these conditions combined to form the cataclysmic fire storms.

Perched atop Henry Pera's new barn in the summer of 1919, Bill Perttula and John Pera take a break while installing roofing. *(Photo courtesy of Rodney Ikola)*

Numerous fires were burning throughout the fall of 1918, partially a result of extensive logging operations that left large tracts of woodland littered with tinder-dry slash. It was one of these fires at Milepost 62 along the Great Northern Railroad near Brookston that appeared to be the main source of the great Cloquet Fire.

On Thursday, October 10, a passenger train stopped at Milepost 62. After its departure, those who stayed behind noticed a small fire burning where the train stopped, but efforts to extinguish it were unsuccessful. The fire smoldered until weather conditions on the 12th, as noted above, caused the blaze to explode into an uncontrollable inferno.

On the day of the fire, Henry Pera was fulfilling part of his obligation for community road work. At that time, in lieu of taxes, farmers would donate their time—and usually the use of their horses—for maintenance of township roads. The day had started looking ominous with smoke filling the air and an eerie glow to the sky. Toward midday Henry told the road supervisor, Charles Pantsari (later Pantsar), that he was going home due to the deteriorating conditions. Henry probably had another reason, too—at the time he did not trust the banks and he had hidden his life savings of $400 in the basement.

As the day wore on, it became apparent that a catastrophe was about to befall the area. When the smoke thickened and sparks began to fall from the sky, Henry ordered his four children at the farm—Hilma, Selma, Elsie and Carl—to run down Marks Road to the small settlement of Harney, about a mile and a quarter to the south. They were joined by neighbor Antti Perttula. As they started down the road, sparks were falling more rapidly and the smoke and wind increased dramatically.

At Harney they gathered with other refugees and waited at the railroad station for arrival of a relief train from Duluth. The train transported them to West Duluth where they walked to the Henry Perttula residence to spend the night. Henry Perttula, a son of Antti and Caroline Perttula, was a former township resident who grew up across the Marks Road from the Pera family.

Henry Pera herded all the animals into the middle of a plowed field and—with the exception of one calf that burned—he managed to extinguish any flames that started from sparks on the animals' fur.

Saving the farm buildings and house was impossible. Henry spent the night with his animals in the plowed field. The next morning, he

A bumper crop of clover in 1920 indicates the fire may have had minimal impact on soil conditions. This photo was taken on the Henry Pera farm; sisters Selma Pera (later Ikola) wields a hayfork while Elsie Pera (Maunu) guides the team.
(Photo courtesy of Rodney Ikola)

brought the animals to the Marks and Barney farms about a mile south on the Marks Road. He was assisted by Emil Kinnunen, whose farm had not burned even though it was straight west of the Pera farm.

Destruction in the area was complete. At least five farms had existed on the one-mile stretch of Marks Road where the Pera farm was located, but after the fire the only building still standing was the outhouse on the Eetu Perttula farm.

For some the fire was especially devastating. The Eetu Perttula family had just finished building a new home, only to see it completely destroyed. Among their animals, only a pig survived. In later years Saima, Eetu's daughter, would recall how they ate bacon all winter.

On the day of the fire, John and Oscar Pera were working at a logging camp on the north shore of Lake Superior near Larsmont. The next day, upon hearing of the fire, they immediately traveled back to Esko to assist in the cleanup and rebuilding efforts.

Hilda Pera was already married to John Luokkala at the time and they lived in a house on what was the Mattson Road (now the Nelson Road). When conditions started to deteriorate, Hilda left with her four small children—Albin, Hannah, Pearl and Oscar—and walked south toward the North Cloquet Road where they spent the night in an empty cabin. The next day they took the train to Duluth (presumably also from Harney). Meanwhile, John lent assistance to the neighboring Holombo brothers, one of whom was blind and the other of limited mental capacity.

Mary was working in West Duluth at a *poikatalo* (men's rooming house) and elected to stay at work in the aftermath of the fire because there was little she could do in the rebuilding efforts.

The four Pera children who spent the night in West Duluth walked to their farm the next day only to see it completely destroyed. One can only imagine the impact this must have had on them. Arrangements were made to obtain temporary living space at the Charles Marks' home, about a mile south along the Marks Road from the original Pera farm. Henry and the children lived upstairs at the Marks' home while their house was being rebuilt; the animals pastured at the Marks and Barney properties.

John and Oscar returned from their logging jobs and took charge of rebuilding the farm. John worked on obtaining building materials, assistance for the family from relief agencies and insurance claims. Oscar took over building construction with the help of Frank Lehto, a local carpenter from Finland. A local stone mason nicknamed "Helsingin Matti" was hired to do the stonework on the new chimneys. This was Oscar's first major building project and it led to a lifetime in the construction industry.

Water was always a problem at the old farmstead so the new farm site was positioned about an eighth of a mile to the north. It was located between two narrow strips of swamp because it was thought that water would be encountered at shallower depths in hand-dug wells. Unfortunately, such was not the case and water would continue to pose problems at the new site.

Rebuilding efforts started immediately after the fire because it was late in the year and shelter had to be provided for the family and animals. Luckily, the fall of 1918 was unusually warm so these tasks could be accomplished before the snow arrived. On the downside, the warm weather continued the drought and numerous small fires were rekindled when the winds increased. One of these fires erupted close to where the new Pera house was being rebuilt and nearly spread to the house before it was contained.

Simultaneous with the house construction, efforts were started to rebuild the barn and other farm buildings. Luckily, an abandoned barn was found and arrangements were made for its purchase. The large timbers that formed the bottom portion of the structure were disassembled and moved to the Pera farm, where they were reassembled for a new upper story and roof.

Years later Selma recalled that her job every day during the rebuilding was to bring coffee from the Marks farm to the workers at the new site at 10 a.m. and 2 p.m. One day while crossing the bridge over the Midway River, she heard whistles start blowing at the surviving mills in Cloquet. Word had been received that the armistice signaling the end of World War I had been reached on November 11, 1918.

When construction at the new farm was completed, neighbors were invited to celebrate the event. Matt Perttula was the first visitor to have coffee in the new house.

CHAPTER 9

'I CAN'T LEAVE WITH BREAD IN THE OVEN'

Excerpts from "A Sunnarborg Saga," submitted by Elvie Kinnunen Gramlich. Elvie's mother was Jennie Sunnarborg (1912-1977), age 6 in 1918. Elvie transcribed this information from a radio documentary written by Dale Kinnunen and broadcast on WKLK. Dale, a 1961 Esko graduate, used his extensive interview of George Sunnarborg (1906-2000) as his source material.

Bits of burning leaves were flying through the air on that October Saturday in 1918. In many ways it was a normal Saturday. The sauna was heating and Jennie Sunnarborg was making the weekly supply of bread for her husband Nels and their 10 children.

The summer had been much drier than normal. Sparks from train engines had started many small fires in the peat bogs and some of the fires had smoldered for many days. On this Saturday the wind was strong and gusty. Nels, 17-year-old John, and Jonas Sommers, the hired man, were showered with ashes as they worked clearing a wooded area in the pasture of their township dairy farm three miles east of Cloquet.

In the afternoon the telephone began to ring incessantly with emergency calls. Houses and barns were burning several miles to the north and the call was out for every able-bodied man and boy to come and help.

Jennie urged John to go and help their neighbors, but he was reluctant. His older brother Charles was away at school, leaving only himself and Jonas to help Nels if their home was endangered. Fourteen- year-old Ed and 12-year-old George were too young to be of much help. The rest of the family consisted of Mary, age 16; Emil, 10; Oscar, 8; Jennie, 6; Henry, 3; and the baby, 13-month-old Irene.

Late in the afternoon neighbor Matt Pykkonen (1870-1961) called and asked John to go with him to fight the fire at Aino Koski's (1892-1965), his son-in-law's home. Matt came to pick up John in his car and just as they were leaving another neighbor, Charles Johnson, ran up and volunteered to go also. It was between 4 and 5 p.m. when they left.

Still standing a century later, this garage at 36 West Harney Road was built as a temporary home by the Nels Sunnarborg family in the fall of 1918. Nine members of the Sunnarborg family lived in the 24x24-foot structure, built from lumber donated by the Red Cross. *(Photo courtesy of Patti Sunnarborg Lockman)*

When the volunteers arrived at Koski's, they were told that help was needed more urgently at the Erick Mattson (1899-1996) farm, so John and Charles went there. They were put to work at saving the barn. Water barrels had been filled earlier in the day and this water was used to extinguish the sparks that landed on the wooden shingles of the house and barn. The barrels were emptied and refilled several times until the well went dry.

The only liquid available was cow urine in the storage tank under the barn. This extremely powerful smelling substance had been saved for use as a fertilizer, but it saved Erik Mattson's house and barn. Due to lack of water and manpower, however, all of the smaller outbuildings were destroyed.

At the Sunnarborg home preparations were made to fight the fire. Nels and the boys filled all available tanks and barrels with water.

Ma and Mary milked the 12 cows and daughter Jennie did her usual chore of drying the silverware after supper.

Ma had put the loaves of bread into the oven and took the younger children to the sauna. Before she finished bathing the children, Pa came and warned her that the fire was getting close. She said she had to finish washing the children. Pa stepped out (of the sauna) and came right back. He said, "We have to get out of here. I'll go get the horses ready."

Pa harnessed the horses, but as he was taking them out of the stable, one of them got spooked and kicked him. By the time he got up off the floor, the horse had run outside. The large wagon was not equipped to be pulled by only one horse, so Pa was forced to take the smaller one-horse buggy. The horse was too nervous to hitch, however, so Pa tied it behind the buggy.

By now the shingles on the house were burning, but Ma said, "I can't leave the house with bread in the oven."

"We can't worry about the bread. All we can worry about is our lives," said Pa.

It was about 7:30 or 8 p.m. when they left the house with nothing but the clothes on their backs, a large piece of canvas and a fur coat. The house door faced north, against the wind. The fire, combined with the strong wind, burned their hair and eyebrows. Ma and the little ones got into the buggy and Pa pulled it himself toward the main road. The lane was steep and the buggy got away, ending up in the ditch on the other side of Harney Road.

"Take the canvas and start walking east to the Midway River," said Pa. "I'll stay here and try to save this horse and buggy."

Ed and George carried the canvas. Ed was singing hymns about the end of the world and how the Lord was coming. Ma carried Irene and she was crying. Everyone was holding hands; the flames and smoke made it impossible to see. There were other people and horses and cattle on the road. Swearing, crying, and screaming could be heard. Ed and George ended up in the Midway River. The rest of the family was taken by wagon to Andrew Tan's (1885-1977) farm by Daniel Tan (1890-1959).

It was about midnight when the Erick Mattson farm was (finally considered) safe…John and Charles started walking home. They were exhausted and their eyes burned from smoke and ashes. The night was cool so they were cold and smelled very bad because their clothes were soaking wet with concentrated cow urine. They were anxious to get home and headed south into the area where the fire was still at its height.

Fire was a flaming cloud over their heads and at times it seemed as if the air itself was burning. Wooden culverts under the road were burning, so they also had fire under their feet. They saw cattle on fire in roadside pastures.

Other people (along the way) begged John and Charles to help them, but the two were exhausted and anxious to get home to learn the fate of their own homes and families. They saw the body of old Mrs. Maki in a ditch. They had to deal with a burning telephone pole that almost fell on them with its tangled wires.

About a half-mile from home, John could see flames where his home had been; a few hundred feet to the south all was intact. Here, to his surprise, he found Pa's buggy. John took the fur coat out of the buggy and lay down on the ground with it to rest.

About 3 a.m. Pa came back to the home site, still leading the horse. Pa and John hitched the horse to the buggy and went east to the river. They found Ed, George and many other wet, cold people sheltered under the canvas that Pa had taken from the barn.

At daybreak Pa decided to head to the Markus home, his father-in-law's farm. He prayed that he would find his wife and younger children there.

About a half-mile to the east they found the Pantsar farmhouse intact, and although no one was home, they went in to rest. John was lying on the floor with the fur coat still on, smelling of cow urine, when some other people came in and wondered what the horrible smell was in the house. John acted as if he didn't hear, and said nothing.

John remembered that after they left the Pantsar home and arrived at the intersection of Church Road, a wagon was seen approaching. It was Sakri Tan (1858- 1931) taking Ma and the children to her parents' home.

All accounts describe the reunion as "joyful."

Pa left to survey the damage to the farm. After a few hours he returned, saying that everything had burned, but the cows had survived.

The family had no place to live and no way to provide shelter and feed for the cows. However, Grandfather Markus's farm had not burned so the Sunnarborgs stayed there for a month.

On Sunday, October 13, a car drove into the yard and the driver announced that the Red Cross had set up a relief office at the Proctor School.

The family returned home the next day to start the clean-up. The hog, a cat and a dog died, but the cows had gone a quarter-mile west. The area was littered with burned boards from a neighbor's house a half mile away.

The Red Cross arranged to secure lumber from a sawmill in Cloquet that had not burned and the family built a 24x24-foot shack to live in. The older boys in the family worked and stayed elsewhere, but there were still nine living in this shed. One bed held three boys. In the winter snow covered the upstairs floor. But the family made it.

Years later George would still laugh at one memory: "I always had hand-me-downs, but just before the fire I got my first pair of brand new overalls. They got burned up in the fire!"

CHAPTER 10

THREE FAMILY STORIES OF SURVIVAL, RECOVERY

Davis Helberg

Pykkonen, originally spelled Pyykkonen: Pronounced correctly, it's one of those jaw-breaker surnames for non-Finnish speakers.

The Finnish pronunciation begins with a hard B sound followed by a soft puff of air that almost sounds like 'poof.," or "BeuK-Konen" (emphasis on the double consonant). A lot of folks just say "Pike-Konen."

So in 1935, when two distantly related Pykkonen families in Thomson Township had sons, and both were named Donald, it wasn't always easy to refer to one or the other without some kind of a qualifier. Who, after all, remembers middle names or initials?

Isaac and Olga (Lumppio) Hill built a log home on West Stark Road in 1905. After the fire destroyed the home and all the family's possessions, they moved to New Hampshire, but they returned in 1919 to build another house on Erkkila Road. *(Photo courtesy of Donald W. Pykkonen)*

The Matt and Olga Pykkonen house and barn at the southwest corner of Canosia and West Harney roads survived the fire and provided temporary lodging—plus a sauna—for many less fortunate neighbors. *(Photo courtesy of Donald W. Pykkonen)*

Ultimately, however, as they reached adulthood, their career choices make it simpler. For years, Donald W. has been known locally as Don the Banker while Donald A. is often called Don the Farmer.

In one sense, they're still tied together because both had grandparents who endured the 1918 Fire and made contributions to the recovery of friends, neighbors and the greater community.

Following is a paraphrased recollection contributed by Don the Banker regarding his grandparents' experiences:

Don's maternal grandparents, Isaac and Olga (Lumppio) Hill, built a log home (see photo) on West Stark Road in about 1905. After the fire struck, Olga and the children spent the night in a potato field while father Isaac helped combat the blaze at a neighbor's home. When Isaac returned the next morning, he found his family alive, but the house and all the family's possessions were gone.

The family chose to move to Olga's brother's home in southern New Hampshire, but six months later they returned to start their lives anew.

They purchased 80 acres on the Erkkila Road where the Red Cross had provided one of its two-room dwellings for fire victims. The building had no indoor plumbing, no sewer, no heating system and no electricity, but the family cut trees for the wood stove, had an oil burner for heat, and hung three kerosene lamps for indoor light. An outdoor toilet was erected behind a newly-built barn. Water for the house came from an outside well and was carried by pail ("running water," according to Don.)

"With the Red Cross housing assistance, and ongoing income from the sale of milk and some crops, the Hill family embarked on a new life together in Thomson Township—a second time," he said.

Meanwhile, Don's paternal grandparents, Matt and Olga Pykkonen, were able to save their house, barn and cattle at the corner of Canosia Road and West Harney Road (see photo). Oldest son Charles and his siblings formed a bucket brigade to keep the fire from consuming the home structures while father Matt helped protect his sister's house a couple miles away.

Afterward, the Pykkonens were among many local farmers who used their homes to provide temporary lodging for those less fortunate.

"Housing was vitally important since the cold winter season was upon them," said Don. "In this case, as in many others, there was an added feature of an outdoor sauna that provided a place for families to not only bathe, but probably a place to contemplate their plans for the family's survival and life in the future."

*   *   *

The story of Don the Farmer Pykkonen's grandparents and their contributions was recorded in the October 2012 edition of The Finnish American Reporter, *published in Hancock, Michigan. It was written by associate editor David Maki and is reprinted here by permission:*

When the tragic fire of October 1918 swept through Cloquet, Minnesota, and nearby communities, many family farms and area businesses were lost to the blaze.

Except for at least one, thanks to the bravery of its owners.

"Most of the area around us burned totally," said Donald Pykkonen, who now owns the family farm in Esko that was established by his grandfather, Kalle. "(But) Grandpa and Grandma [Briita] stayed here; she wet the sacks and he kept the roofs from starting on fire.

"Their determination was that 'if this burns, we're going to go, too."

As a result, several of the Pykkonen farm buildings survived the fire...

Donald himself wasn't yet born at the time the fire ravaged the community, but he recalls hearing stories about the fire and its after-effects.

"I always remember when people would come over they'd have stories about the fire," he said. "As soon as I was able to comprehend, I'd hear those stories."

One of the community's stories involves the Pykkonen family directly. As a result of the fire's enormity, many lives were lost—the resulting number of bodies necessitated makeshift morgues, one of which ended up being the Pykkonen barn [Ed. Note: The building was actually a *riihi*, a grain-drying shed.].

Donald's grandmother, since she had a background in midwifery, took part in preparing the bodies for burial, Donald believes. Most, if not all, of the deceased were of Finnish descent and were likely buried in the cemetery at the end of the Pykkonen property.

The barn still stands today, though Donald laments that it's begun to show signs of its age (see photo).

"It's beginning to lean, and we need to straighten it out,' he said. "It's full of all my dad's horse machinery, mowers, potato diggers, that type of thing."

In the aftermath of the 1918 Fire, though, the barn was filled with the bodies of deceased neighbors and friends, as funeral directors had limited options for sites, both because of the number of structures destroyed and the number of neighbors who perished.

It's a part of the barn's history that could be considered haunting by some, but Donald sees things from a different perspective.

"It's not a bad feeling to me," he said. "My family was able to help the community in a time of need. That's how my grandpa viewed it, too. He was really a strong Christian person (and) a positive attitude is what he had.

"If the barn really served a purpose, I feel positive about it."

This grain-drying shed, or *riihi*, on Church Avenue served as a temporary morgue in the days immediately after the fire. The farm was established in 1893 by Kalle and Briita Pykkonen and is owned today by grandson Donald A. Pykkonen and his wife, Ardie. The township's only other surviving *riihi* is at the Esko Historical Society Museum. *(Photo by Davis Helberg)*

* * *

Finally, the following memories of Antti (Andrew) Pykkonen (1864-1973), father of Don the Farmer, are from an article "65 years in One Home" written by Dr. J. E. Nopola, former pastor of St. Matthews Lutheran Church in *Lutheran Voice* magazine 1969,

When asked what about his most trying experience, Antti spoke of the great fire of 1918. On that fateful October day, he hitched his team to the wagon. Twenty-four people climbed hastily into the wagon box and Antti headed into the thick smoke to deliver his family and neighbors from the flames.

About a mile from home the horses lost the road in the smoke, the wagon box and the people tumbled into the roadside, and all seemed lost. The box was thrown back on the wagon and the riders climbed in to continue their flight. But within another mile the fire met them with such fury that they had no choice but to turn back.

Taking another road the band came to a bridge crossing the river. There they spent the night and found to their joy the next morning the prospects of survival were much brighter.

Upon returning home Antti found to his surprise the house and barn standing on the homestead among the smoldering ruins of the neighborhood and the burnt carcasses of the cattle.

CHAPTER 11

'I CRIED FOR MANY YEARS AFTERWARD'

Saima Anttila Lumppio (1910-2001), from "Saima's Story, The Fire that Changed My Life." Additional details are an audio tape at the Carlton County Historical Society, part of the Carlton County Cooperative Oral History Project. Saima was the daughter of Charles and Nannie Anttila and lived on the Erkkila Road.

I was 8 years old, but I can remember just about everything that happened that day...

The wind was blowing hard and things were flying around. The sky was dark and we could see a glow of light far away from our home. We didn't know what it was, and later when the wind turned (from the) north, we knew it must be something serious.

My mother and older brother Hans were milking cows. They let the cows out of the barn because they knew something serious was happening. At that point, our dad was fighting fires at the neighbors. When he noticed the wind turned north, he hurried home. He made it just in time to help us...just before the porch collapsed because our house was on fire. There was no way to get out of the house except through a window. Dad knocked the window out and pulled all of us out. It was a terrible feeling to face the sparks, burning wood and trees.

We all ran to the road. Dad told us to go in the ditch for fresh air. It was smoky and getting dark. We ducked into a ditch every few feet. The fifth and last time we went into the ditch, two huge bundles of hay from our neighbor's hayshed flew on top of my younger sister and me. We struggled unsuccessfully to get out from under that burning hay. The rest of the family didn't know what had happened to us, and they continued running toward a bridge. The bridge spanned a small creek (Crystal Creek) that ran under the North Road.

Suddenly, Dad noticed that two of his children were missing. He quickly ran back. He discovered my younger sister Lila pulling me to safety because I had already lost consciousness.

My dad picked us up and carried each of us under an arm to the safety underneath the bridge.

There were several people under the bridge. The older people thought that it would be better to go to the school house across the road for shelter—but then that started burning, too. Then they decided to go to the neighbor's potato field. The buildings there had already burned so it seemed safe from fiery disaster.

We all went to the potato fields. I remember my younger sister and I were really in terrible pain. We were burned very badly. The fiery hay had burned our legs, hair, arms, faces and my side. We were safe for a little while in the potato field. The older people must have felt unsure about the safety of the potato field because they searched nearby and discovered a little farm that hadn't burned. They all decided to go and save it because then the women and children could be inside. There were many families in that little house. The men and older boys kept putting water on the house and saved it.

That night I recall we all tried to sleep. I remember that it was impossible because I was in so much pain. In the morning, somebody went to the cheese factory about four miles away to get help. I still don't know who went to the Bohren's cheese factory on the Antilla road to get help; I guess my sister and I were in too much pain to remember. We had gallon-sized blisters on our legs and on my side.

My entire family minus brother Hans (who stayed at the cheese factory) went to Duluth to the armory. We stayed there for about three days. Dad said I was unconscious. Finally my sister Lila and I were moved to St. Luke's Hospital into a small room. They clipped our clothes off with scissors because they were so badly burned on our skin. After that we moved into a children's ward. Someone cut our hair because it was almost all burned off.

The next day the hospital staff started our treatments. They were horrible. Every morning they tried to clean our bloody scars which were dirty with dirt from the potato field. They didn't have any medication to stop the pain or the bleeding. One day they put on cotton batting on the open sores, and the next morning they would take it off and put warm paraffin wax on. I was in terrible pain.

I recall crying… each morning after the treatments. The doctor who treated me was really nice. He told me "If I don't do this (remove the

bandages for the wax treatment) for you, I'll have to cut your legs off."
Lila and I stayed at St. Luke's hospital for five months.

The fire affected more than just our bodies. During our prolonged stay in the hospital, both my mother and brother George died from influenza. My sister and I missed the rest of that school year. It was very difficult to catch up when we went back to school in the fall.

When my sister and I were finally released from the hospital in the spring of 1919, we found out we didn't have a home. We went to my auntie's, my father's sister's house on the Reservation Road. We didn't get to go home until Dad built a little house. It was very sad to go home…no Mother, no toys, no little kids to play with. I cried for many years afterward.

CHAPTER 12

FAMILY BIBLE SURVIVED

C. Philip Johnson

With thick smoke, howling wind and flames rapidly approaching their farm on the corner of North Cloquet and Erickson Roads, Priita Johnson and her daughter Ida had to run for their lives.

Priita had waited until the last moment, hoping the menfolk would return and fight the fire. But her husband Nels had left earlier in the afternoon to try to stop the fire by the St. Louis River north of Cloquet.

So, like many of their neighbors, Priita and Ida ran down the hill to the Midway River. For some reason Priita carried the thick family Bible, written in Finnish. Halfway to the river, the two were nearly overcome by smoke, and Priita dropped the Bible in the hayfield, grabbed Ida's hand and reached the river before the flames overtook them.

They spent all night in the water. Early the next morning they walked up the hill. Halfway up the slope was a small grassy spot. In the middle of that patch of unburned ground sat the Bible, its cover charred but otherwise intact.

Handed down through the generations, the blackened book is a reminder of Priita and Ida's race for survival a century ago.

The morning after the fire, Priita Johnson and her daughter, Ida, found the Finnish Bible that Priita dropped when they raced to the Midway River for refuge. Except for some charring on the cover as evident on the right side, the book was intact.
(Photo by C. Philip Johnson)

CHAPTER 13

RESPITE IN A POTATO FIELD

Robert Lindquist, a 1985 Esko graduate now residing in the Twin Cities, submitted this story based on conversations with his great-aunt, Sophie (Lindquist) Johnson. Said Lindquist: "[She] was my best friend growing up. She was 70 years old when I was born. I spent many years in my youth mowing her lawn. After the work was done, I spent hours talking with and listening to Sophie's stories about Thomson Township, the Lindquist family and the 1918 Fire. Her mind was sharp until her passing at the young age of 105."

Sophie (Lindquist) Johnson as a 22-year-old was married to William "Bill" Johnson, living in Cloquet with 4-month-old daughter Ruth Johnson. Sophie got a ride from a friend to her parents, John and Hannah Lindquist, who homesteaded on the northern side of Thomson Township the day of the fire. Bill stayed behind to fight the fires. Upon arriving at her parents, the smoke was getting thicker by the moment. Sophie was told by her mother to take Ruth to her in-laws, the Johnsons.

The Johnson family lived one mile south of the Lindquist farm. The harrowing walk to the Johnsons was challenging for Sophie and her infant daughter Ruth. The smoke was so thick she barely could see in front of her. Once at the Johnsons, they hurried to load their automobile and off they went to the village of Thomson to the south, where they hoped was a safe place to go. As they were leaving, their barn burst in to flames, but the Johnson family, Sophie and Ruth made it to Thomson safely.

Back at the Lindquist Farm, Sophie's parents, John and Hannah, and her younger siblings, Henry 18, Martha 13 and Ted 12, were gathering valuables to bury in a potato field just west of the house. John let the horses and cattle out of the barn to fend for themselves. Their two older sons, Charles and Eero, in their yearly 20s, were not living at the farm at the time. Hannah also had her children put their "Sunday Best" clothing into the car.

The fire was getting too close for the family to escape, so the Lindquist family laid themselves in the potato field for protection. After some time had passed, Hannah told Henry to check on the house and barn. It was evening. When Henry got close enough to see the barn, it was ablaze. The barn had been built that summer and was full of hay for the cattle and horses for the months ahead. In front of the new barn was the old barn, also in flames.

Henry made his way past the log home to the new house, built in 1913, and found it was still standing. He entered the front porch to find a box of brand new Sears & Roebuck underwear smoldering. After tossing out the box, Henry made his way to the potato field to let the family know it was safe to return.

The next morning they found the new barn, the old barn, the sauna and the car were all destroyed. The only buildings to survive were the old log home and the new house. That morning the men went looking for the cattle and horses. The horses made it through but the cows did not fare well because their udders were badly burned. That winter the family used the old log home for the barn to house the cattle and the horses.

The fire left Sophie and Bill Johnson with nothing but the clothes on their backs, as their house in Cloquet burned. Bill's parents also lost much of what they owned, but at least they still had their home. Just to the north of the Lindquist farm were the Forstie and Winquist farms; both were untouched. To the east on the adjacent 40, the Maunu School had burned to the ground.

CHAPTER 14

DID HARNEY BURN?

Rodney Ikola

In the immediate aftermath of the fire, communication with the devastated areas was impossible to chaotic at best. Most of the reports came from survivors who streamed into Duluth and Superior by the hundreds and thousands.

Many of these survivors came as passengers on rescue trains sent into the impacted area by the Duluth Winnipeg & Pacific Railroad (DW&P). Many of them boarded the trains at Harney, so the reports tended to concentrate on events that occurred in the Harney vicinity (the junction of Harney and Marks roads).

For several days, newspaper accounts contained headlines such as "only 50 saved at Harney" (one account purportedly said only 20 were saved), implying everyone else in the Harney vicinity had succumbed. Other accounts described the vast destruction of buildings in and around the little community. Undoubtedly most of these events were reported by survivors who fled to Harney to catch a relief train and described events in the area to the north from which they had fled.

In fact, no buildings were destroyed at Harney and no lives were lost. At its closest point, the fire came within three-quarters of a mile, burning along the north side of Midway River. The farms between Harney and Midway River were not touched by the fire; moreover, they provided shelter for many of the families displaced from north of the river.

These early reports were subsequently corrected by the media but first impressions have a stubborn resistance to change. Even today, 100 years later, occasional mention of the devastation at Harney can be found in accounts of the fire.

Ed. Note: Reinforcing the point that Harney did not burn, there's also this excerpt from *Esko's Corner, An Illustrated History of Esko and Thomson Township*, regarding Juntti's store in Harney:

The Harney Depot became a gathering point for residents awaiting the arrival of Duluth Winnipeg & Pacific rescue trains. The DW&P, now part of the Canadian National, built the depot after completing its line from Virginia to Duluth in 1912. The depot depicted here was later replaced by a larger building that served the area until 1961.
(Esko Historical Society photo)

"The event that solidified Juntti's place in the community… was the great October 1918 Fire. That night, when the store and upstairs living quarters seemed doomed, Eino and Jenni Juntti and their children fled the building and sought refuge at the Midway River. The next day, on discovering their store intact, Eino and Jenni opened the warehouse and dispensed goods and materials 'without distinction to the penniless who had lost everything. They gave thousands of dollars' worth of building supplies and necessities of life…Without their generosity and trust, many a person's lot would have been much more difficult.'"

CHAPTER 15

RESCUE AND RELIEF; ORDER OUT OF CHAOS

C. Philip Johnson

Despite the scope of the fire and its sudden unexpected appearance, rescue and relief efforts sprang up immediately. This rapid response is described in a report by the Home Guard's chief medical officer, 1st Lieutenant J.R. Manley (the Home Guard, established during World War 1, was a volunteer force under the command of the state governor):

"Late Saturday afternoon, October 12, 1918, and in the early evening of the same day, refugees began to come into Duluth from the burned forest fire districts. It became necessary to organize hurriedly some headquarters where they could be inspected, the degree of medical or surgical care necessary determined, and either treated or sent for treatment to one of the hospitals or other improvised places.

"This process rapidly developed into a huge undertaking. The third or dormitory floor of the [Duluth] Armory became congested and it became necessary to utilize the main or drill floor of the armory to accommodate them. This was done by placing cots in long rows on the drill floor. About six or eight or more of these rows of cots were occupied by refugees during the first night. The third floor, containing 50 to 75 cots, was converted into a temporary hospital in which the burned and sick cases were housed for the night and during Sunday. One or two labor (confinement) cases were transferred to hospitals for care. During the evening the physicians were called to the armory to render emergency services and they responded promptly and gratuitously. A staff of nurses was organized and physicians placed in charge of a dispensary ...

"After the immediate emergency of Saturday night and Sunday was passed, the following steps were taken to bring order out of partial chaos. After the inspection of various public buildings which had been hastily converted into quarters for refuges, i.e., Shrine Auditorium, Masonic Temple, Court House and in the West End, the Irving and Denfeld Schools (the two latter facilities housing the tuberculosis patients, brought in during Saturday night from Nopeming), notes were made on the total bed capacity. It was necessary to utilize the armory for a

With Duluth and Superior hospitals overflowing, the Duluth Armory, built in 1915, was designated as an emergency hospital and Home Guard headquarters. Several other facilities, including schools and churches, also became havens for refugees.
(Photo from "The Fury and the Flames," 1919)

central headquarters and the main floor was especially desirable for that purpose at once.

"Several churches in the city fitted out their basements with beds and bedding and cooking and feeding facilities and quickly made ready to care for 500 refugees. The armory main floor was therefore soon evacuated and made available for headquarters purposes. Those persons ill or burned were placed where physicians were in attendance.

"On Monday the 14th, at 10 o'clock, an emergency meeting of the St. Louis County Medical Society was called at St. Mary's Hospital [and] a memorandum was made of available time which each physician present would give to the work of relief of refugees. From this list a schedule was made of all physicians who would give gratuitously of their time to this very important work."

People who were running for their lives a day earlier started to return on October 13 to assess the damage and find family and friends.

Both the Home Guard and the National Guard, under federal control due to the war, provided transportation to the fire area as well as security. Two of the Home Guard units were Motor Corps and guardsmen who used their own cars, as well as other private vehicles, to begin moving relief supplies to outlying areas, rescuing survivors, and searching for bodies.

By October 13 the Duluth Chapter of the Red Cross was fully involved. An emergency hospital was established in the Duluth Armory; more than 400 injury cases were treated in the first 24 hours. Cooks from the guard units served hot meals nonstop for nearly 3,000 refugees. Serious burn victims were transferred to area hospitals. Further complicating the situation was the outbreak of the Spanish Flu; pictures of the armory show many individuals wearing flu masks.

The Red Cross also became a clearinghouse organization. Workers made every effort to register survivors and their addresses. These lists were printed in local newspapers enabling family members to locate those who were separated while fleeing the fires.

Minnesota Governor Joseph A.A. Burnquist visited the fire area on October 14. The scope of the fire necessitated a special emergency government agency, so the Minnesota Commission of Public Safety formed the Minnesota Forest Fires Relief Commission.

This new commission met on October 17 and began to coordinate all rescue and relief efforts and plan for both short term (food and clothing) and long term (shelter) relief. More than 50,000 people needed help. The commission established substations in outlying areas. The *Duluth News Tribune* listed the "Finnish church on the Cloquet Road near Harney" [St. Matthews Lutheran] as the township's substation where residents—the paper numbered them in one report as 80 and in a later story as 155 families—accepted first aid supplies, groceries, clothing and animal feed.

Families who lost their homes applied to the Red Cross for one of two types of temporary housing—a 12x16-foot shelter for small families and a 12x20-foot shelter for larger families. By mid-November dozens of these ersatz homes dotted the township.

Farmers also had to provide shelter and feed for surviving livestock.

The commission provided additional building materials and feed for cattle. Materials for rebuilding came primarily by rail. By October 26, the Duluth, Winnipeg and Pacific had repaired all the burned area bridges—one between Harney and Nopeming and five between Harney and Taft.

Although most of the city of Cloquet was destroyed by the fire, the death toll—said to be no more than four—could have been much worse. Rescue trains dispatched from Duluth carried between 7,000 and 8,000 people to safety.
(Carlton County Historical Society photo)

CHAPTER 16

NOPEMING EVACUATED

C. Philip Johnson

As the fire spread eastward, officials in Duluth, including the fire department and members of the Home Guard under the command of Major Roger M. Weaver, responded. Hundreds of volunteers worked to evacuate survivors west of Duluth and backfires were lit on the Duluth hillside to stop the flames.

One area of concern was the Nopeming Sanatorium. The Sanatorium, lying on a hillside just east of Thomson Township (partially visible today east of I-35 on "Nopeming Hill"), treated tuberculosis victims and was deliberately isolated from populated areas.

Home Guard efforts to evacuate the TB patients are vividly described in a letter to Major Weaver from Dr. E.L. Tuohy of the sanatorium. Excerpts of the letter:

"Possibility of danger from the fire to the Sanatorium was first realized about 7 o'clock…At 9 o'clock when we attempted to get in touch with the Canadian Northern Railway, to get a train out there, the matter seemed…more acute.

"It was said that the bridges were burned out and that the train could not get there. At 10 o'clock the men (Home Guard)…were willing to attempt to reach the institution by auto. The writer, together with Mr. Elmer Whyte, was in the first car to arrive at the institution about 11 o'clock.

"By a curious freak of the wind and by the position of the hill just back of the institution, the flames were then burning around the institution, and it looked as though it (the fire) might pass by. The first temptation was to not attempt the hazard of moving the patients out, but to fight the fire and save the institution.

"However, the great series of cars began to flock in so rapidly that a removal of the patients seemed possible. It is a fine tribute to the service of the Home Guard and the Motor Division to realize that the entire capacity of the institution, 192, many of them very ill, together with at

Nearly 200 patients and 50 attendants were safely evacuated from Nopeming Sanitorium on the night of the fire. Nopeming opened in 1912 as the state's first tuberculosis hospital. It was converted to a nursing home in 1971 and closed in 2002. It is now open to public tours. *(Photo from www.nopeming.com)*

least 40 or 50 more attendants, were successfully and easily removed from the institution, and were down in the two high schools in West Duluth by 1 o'clock.

"Car after car came quietly, and without commotion the very sick patients were placed in the laps of others in the rear seats of the cars and the cars went off down the road without an accident.

"Later in the night, and for succeeding days, a detachment of the Home Guard remained to control the fire, and the fact that an institution of a value of $300,000 was saved for St. Louis County is proof enough of the efficiency of your work…"

CHAPTER 17

EINAR REPONEN: SADLY SYMBOLIC

Davis Helberg

"AD 1918—the Year of Sorrows—has gone; and most of us saw it go with few regrets. The year that saw the culmination of the butchery of the World War; the deadly plague of influenza; the appalling casualty lists from overseas that we dreaded to see and could not help trembling with cold fear lest a loved name appeared therein; the awful avalanche of flames that swept this part of our state, leaving Cloquet a blackened waste and making many of our wooded districts of this county a smoking charnel—lives, homes, property wiped out in a breath of fire in a fleeting hour of horror. Yes, it was a year of sorrows and the only bright spot was that the war ended."

Einar Reponen *(From Ancestry.com, posted in 2013 by Mark Hintsa)*

As vividly and emotionally described above in the *Cloquet Pine Knot's* opening 1919 editorial, 1918 has been characterized as a year of three tragedies—the World War (not yet known as World War I), the Spanish influenza and, for northeastern Minnesota, the great Cloquet fire.

In a sense, Einar Reponen's brief life symbolized all three.

Reponen came from Finland as a 9-year-old in 1902. As a young man he was drafted into the Army. Stationed at Camp Grant, Rockford, Illinois, he succumbed to "Spanish flu" on October 7, 1918. His body was sent home for burial; the casket arrived at the Cloquet train depot and was placed on the platform for the family to claim—on October 12.

Unfortunately, the 1918 Fire swept through town that day. Reponen's body was partially burned, but enough of his remains were intact so there could be a proper funeral and burial.

Einar, whose nephew Gerald Reponen spent most of his childhood years in Esko (graduating class of 1947), still rests in the Sawyer Cemetery, just west of Sawyer off Highway 210.

CHAPTER 18

UP FROM THE ASHES: A NEW SCHOOL SYSTEM

C. Philip Johnson

Prior to October 12, local students were served by 10 one- or two-room schoolhouses, including one west of the township line in Scanlon and one near the township's southernmost tip in Forbay. Three of the northern schools—all on or near North Cloquet Road—were destroyed by the fire.

Afterward, students attended classes in the still intact schools in the southern part of the township and at the town hall and at the Finnish Lutheran Church (now St. Matthews Lutheran). The church was at the corner of North Cloquet and Church roads and had barely escaped the fire.

Township residents, led by newly arrived school superintendent A. L. Winterquist, now reevaluated the one-room school model and decided to consolidate all the schools. In January 1919 the community voted 52 to 9 to form an independent school district so the township could eventually have a high school. It would be known as Town of Thomson Consolidated District 1.

A proposal for one school centrally located on the top of the hill just north of the present township garage on Canosia Road was voted down. A revised bond issue calling for two schools, Washington in the north and Lincoln in the south, passed in April 1919.

The township also received $2,109.03 from the state legislature to assist in rebuilding. Having two schools may seem strange from a modern perspective until one reads accounts of the difficulty of travel. Unless students were within walking distance, they rode in horse-drawn buses or, in the winter, sleighs. Students living near the township's outer boundaries could spend at least an hour or two each morning just getting to school, followed by equally long trips home in the afternoon.

By the late fall of 1920 both schools were open and, for the first time, students were able to acquire high school diplomas. Prior to 1920, none of the one-room schools offered more than eight years, although an

With the exception of the low structure on the far right, this was the front view of
Lincoln School as it would have appeared from the highway in the fall of 1920.
The low wing on the right was a gymnasium, added in 1936.
(Photo from 1940 Esko yearbook, "The Lincoln Log")

eighth-grade education was generally considered adequate at the time,
especially in rural areas.

The new Washington School, designed to accommodate Grades
1 through 6, was on the northwest corner of the intersection of the
Canosia and North Cloquet road. It operated until 1980 by which time
all elementary classes had been moved to the Winterquist School in
Esko. The building is now privately owned and has been converted into
residential apartments.

The new Lincoln School (see photo) included the high school and
was on the present location of the school campus at the southeast corner
of Thomson Road and Old Highway 61. The first graduating class in
1921 had one student, Hilda Esko. She was already 20 years old because
the fire had interrupted her studies. There were three graduates in 1922,
then 12 in 1923.

During construction of the Lincoln School—and evidently in
anticipation of its opening—local entrepreneur Alex Esko and his son,
Fritz, built a general store on the west side of Thomson Road, directly

opposite the school. It was this store, and this intersection, that ultimately spawned the name "Esko's Corner," eventually reduced to Esko.

Thus it was the fire, followed by the decision to create a new school district, followed by location of the Lincoln School, that led to the beginning of a small commercial center and the creation of a community. One can only speculate about where and how the community might have developed were it not for the fire.

When fire swept into the township, many of the men were either fighting fires elsewhere or working at distant logging camps. Such was the case at the Joshua Johnson farm near the west end of Sunnarborg Road. Consequently, 13-year-old John S. Hendrickson, shown here, drove his grandmother (Mrs. Johnson), his mother (Hilma Hendrickson) and an aunt to safety in one of the cars in the background. When they returned, the house was standing but the barn and animals had all perished.
(Photo courtesy of John C. Hendrickson)

CHAPTER 19

TOWNSHIP DAMAGES
LOSS OF PUBLIC PROPERTIES

C. Philip Johnson

The scope of the fire was beyond anything a small township government could possibly handle, but Thomson Township did what it could.

The township supervisors at the time—Nels G. Johnson, J.E. Sunnarborg and Peter Hiukka—and Town Clerk John Sota Jr. summarized the damages at a January 2, 1919, meeting, listing the materials below:

Items Lost or Destroyed	Value
29 culverts burned @$8.00 each	$232.00
600 feet burned on Polo Road	$198.25
200 feet burned on road west of Harney Station	$60.00
30 feet span wooden bridges on Proctor Road	$500.00
Town tool and machine shed Section 14	$150.00
1 - 8 horse graders	$300.00
3 road plows	$60.00
24 shovels	$24.00
Total damages	$1,524.25

On March 22, 1919, Supervisors Sunnarborg, Emil Mattinen and Matt Koski, as well as Clerk Daniel Tan, noted that burned cattle needed to be buried, that disposing of their carcasses needed to be done before spring and summer's heat.

A rather curious entry in the Township minutes from the March 1, 1923, annual meeting lists a Supervisors Account of the following: "Received from Railroad Administration—Fire loss: $717." Did the Township take an early offer of the Railroad Administration Board and settle for a fraction of what the damages actually were?

Perhaps the Township reconsidered its settlement, as is suggested by an entry in the minutes of October 5, 1935: "A motion was made by Supervisor Emil Niemi and seconded by Supervisor Joseph Davidson that Chairman of the Board Emil A. Mattinen and Clerk Einar W. Koivisto be hereby empowered and directed to file a verified claim against the U.S. of America, pursuant to private law #336 approved August 27, 1935, by the 74th Congress. Motion carried."

It was prepared on a multipage federal form. Its official name was "Verified Claim Against United States of America Railroad Administration for Property Damage From Fires of October 12, 1918." Although it specifically did not cover personal injury or death, it had pages for a claimant to list damage to buildings, standing timber, asked the claimant for the legal description of his homestead, had a schedule to complete for all personal property items lost, with a value when new, year when it was new, value before the fire and the amount of damage by fire.

On these pages every item of personal property was listed, including furniture, bedding, clothing, books and everything in the house and buildings. Another section required the claimant to list similar information for buildings beside the house damaged or destroyed by the fires, and to draw a small schematic diagram of the farmstead with each building and its location. A section titled, "Other land damage," could include destroyed or damaged fences. If the claimant had any private insurance, that needed to be listed also.

A year later, at an October 7, 1936, meeting, there was an entry referring to the costs of preparation of the form. John Mattinen of Cloquet made out the claim and charged the township $110. However, it was recorded that after "some discussion" the board moved to reduce his payment to $55, which Mattinen accepted.

The supervisors were also counting on the fire settlement monies for other types of funding, as revealed by minutes from a special meeting on December 18, 1935, in Clerk Koivisto's office: "Motion by Supervisor Joseph Davidson seconded by Supervisor Emil Niemi to send Mrs. Raina on the expense of the township to Minnesota State Sanatorium providing Mr. Matt Raina will reimburse the Township when he receives the Fire Money."

Rewriting Insurance Claims

C. Philip Johnson

Some township residents had insured their property with the Finnish Farmers Mutual Insurance Company (later the Esko Mutual Fire Insurance Company). Unfortunately, the company's records, stored in private homes, were all destroyed by the fire.

To solve the problem, members of the company's board of directors simply visited each policy holder to sit down and rewrite policies and their amounts from memory. The loss to the local company was overwhelming. Of the $316,326 of insurance in force at the time, $105,401 in insured property was destroyed, representing a 34 percent loss.

At the state level, the Commissioner of Insurance convened a special committee to organize a way to collect monies to aid northern Minnesota insurance companies. The committee asked the members of all farmers' mutual insurance providers elsewhere in Minnesota to contribute 75 cents for every $1,000 of insurance carried by them in their companies.

Without the aid of insurance companies across the state, the Esko company could not have survived. Local policyholders were also assessed 1½ percent of their policies to help pay for their neighbors' losses.

The concept of reinsurance—whereby small township mutuals contribute to a common fund to help one another withstand large losses—evolved into the creation in 1931 of the Farm Mutual Reinsurance Association (FMRA). Originally based in Herman, Minnesota, its headquarters were moved to Esko in 1949 by Thomson Township native Emil Johnson, FMRA president since 1935.

When Emil Johnson retired in 1962, his son Clifford E. Johnson became corporate secretary. In 1967, FMRA changed its name to the Reinsurance Company of Minnesota (now the RAM Mutual Insurance Company). For a number of years RAM and Esko Mutual shared a small building next to the high school. In 1969, RAM acquired the building from Esko Mutual, which changed its name to Woodland Mutual and moved to Carlton. In 2018, RAM constructed a 22,000-square-foot office complex a mile east of Esko on Highway 61.

CHAPTER 20

A 17-YEAR LEGAL ODYSSEY

C. Philip Johnson

Survivors soon were asking why and how the fire started. Who was to blame?

Many believed the railroads were responsible, and within a few months multiple law suits had been filed. A Forest Fire Investigation Committee was formed by Governor Joseph A.A. Burnquist and held hearings in November. The report did name the railroads as partially responsible, but basically attributed the fire with its tornadic winds to an act of God.

Given that the federal government had nationalized the railroads because of the war effort, lawsuits named both the railroads and the National Railroad Administration. Many local lawyers filed suits on a contingency fee basis. Initial court cases were settled in favor of the railroads; nevertheless, more than 15,000 cases were eventually filed in the next few years.

These cases received a legal boost from a 1920 Minnesota Supreme Court ruling in Jacob Anderson v. Minneapolis, St. Paul & Sault Ste. Marie Railway Company and Others. The court said neither high winds, other fire sources, nor any other act of God could excuse the railroads from their liability.

Members of the Railroad Administration were divided, with some willing to pay for damages when the circumstances were clear. The majority, however, felt that quickly settling a few cases would open the floodgates and result in costs in the millions. Lawyers for Cloquet residents and the commission agreed to have a panel of five district court judges decide the suit brought by A.R. Peterson, a Cloquet resident, against the commission. Four of the five judges agreed with the plaintiff—the fire which destroyed Cloquet was caused by the railroad at Milepost 62.

The rulings in the Jacob Anderson and the Cloquet cases seemed to offer hope to claimants. Trying each individual case would take decades, however, so the district court judges in the Cloquet case, along with Senator Knute Nelson and Eleventh District Judge William Cant, urged the U.S. Congress and the Railroad Administration to form a commission or commissions to hear and settle the claims.

This suggestion became a political football. James Davis, a lawyer who formerly had represented the Railroad Administration, was now its director general. Davis, with Minnesota Senator Frank Kellogg, met with President Warren Harding in July 1929. After the meeting Davis reported to Minnesota Governor Jacob Preus that the federal government would adjust (pay) the fire claims on a fair basis. This "fair basis" was a mere 50 percent settlement. Despite the favorable rulings in Minnesota Supreme Court cases, Cloquet and area residents could therefore recover only half of their losses.

The only recourse township residents now had was to petition Congress for relief, so they joined a lobbying group, the Minnesota Forest Fire Reimbursement Association. This group, led by Cloquet lawyer Frank Yetka, persuaded Eighth District Congressman William Carss (later succeeded by William Pittenger) and Senator Henrik Shipstead to introduce a bill to pay fire victims for their losses—the previously unpaid 50 percent balance.

The "Pittenger Bill" was the subject Congressional hearings in March 1930. James Davis was the first witness. He argued that the 1918 Fire was a natural event, that the large number of subsequent lawsuits were due to greedy lawyers, that the 50 percent cash settlement was fair, and that the Railroad Administration always denied its liability.

Minnesota Congressman William Pittenger, left, and Senator Henrik Shipstead led an arduous political battle to get adequate compensation for fire survivors.
(Public Domain photos)

Davis also worked behind the scenes to kill the bill. Both President Herbert Hoover and his administrative assistant, Walter H. Newton, were sympathetic to Davis' views.

Several people testified in favor of the Pittenger bill. Judge Herbert Dancer, one of the five judges in the Peterson case, castigated Davis. Dancer argued that Davis had no right to ignore Minnesota law and the state supreme court cases which clarified it. Three local attorneys as well as local citizens also testified.

One interesting witness was Anna Dickie Olesen, a fire victim. Her husband was the superintendent of schools in Cloquet at the time of the fire. Olesen was a well-known Chautauqua speaker and gave a riveting first-person account of escaping the flames.

The hearings seemed to bear fruit because the House Committee on Claims approved an amended bill and stated that justice would be served by paying the balance.

The Hoover administration, however, continued to drag its feet. Appeals to the president were sent to the secretary of the treasury and to the assistant director of the Railroad Administration who

Anna Dickie Olesen of Cloquet helped get President Roosevelt's support for fire victim compensation.
(Carlton County Historical Society photo)

agreed with James Davis. As a result, the bill did not pass the House. Congressman Pittenger reintroduced his bill to a new Congress in December 1931. New hearings were set, but once again House members were split and the legislation died.

Progress was made more difficult by the Depression, yet Frank Yetka and Anna Olesen of the Forest Fire Reimbursement Association were not about to give up the fight. Hoping for a favorable reception from President Franklin D. Roosevelt and the New Deal Democrats, Senator Shipstead and newly elected Congressman Einar Hoidale introduced companion bills in March and April 1933.

This time Anna Olesen decided to make a personal appeal to Eleanor Roosevelt; Olesen felt it would result in a direct appeal to FDR. Indeed, FDR handed the case to Attorney General Homer Cummings who concluded that the government had a moral obligation to look further into the claims.

Nonetheless, the administration's favorable view of the fire claims did not lead to immediate legislative solutions. A prolonged and contentious debate in the House ended with a 64 to 44 vote to kill the Hoidale bill.

In 1934 William Pittenger regained his Eighth District House seat. He, along with Congressmen Paul Kvale and Elmer Ryan, introduced three house bills to obtain compensation. Senator Shipstead introduced a companion bill in the Senate which quickly passed. Since Ryan was the lone Democrat, it was felt his bill would have the best chance of passing, and it was attached to the omnibus claims bill of 1935. That piece of legislation finally passed and FDR signed it on August 27, 1935.

To pay the claims after a 17-year delay was a challenge. The Treasury Department unearthed the Railroad Administration's 50 percent settlement records and began to locate the claimants. The first checks were sent out in mid-November 1935.

Although one can only imagine the euphoria when township residents received checks for thousands of dollars in the depths of the Depression, their joy must have been tempered by the knowledge that many claimants died long before Congress finally accepted responsibility.

THE WRITERS AND RESEARCHERS

(See photos on back cover)

Davis Helberg: He became a Great Lakes sailor after graduating from Esko High School in 1958 and spent most of his career in the maritime industry before retiring in 2003 as Duluth port director. Davis also was a newspaper reporter for six years and a columnist for various magazines for more than 30 years. A grandson of Finnish immigrants, he resides with his wife Stacey in his family home.

Rodney Ikola: A 1957 Esko graduate, he continued his education at the Universities of Minnesota (Minneapolis), Minnesota Duluth and Utah. He earned degrees in geology, mathematics and geophysics and spent 56 years evaluating natural resources on six continents. Rodney's father was a Finnish immigrant and his mother was the daughter of native-born Finns. He and his wife Darlene reside in Hibbing.

Connie Jacobson: Connie and her husband, Clarence Sharpe, moved to Esko in 1981. A 1969 Hermantown graduate, she holds multiple degrees from the University of Minnesota, Minneapolis, and Minnesota Duluth. She worked in St. Louis County government for 33 years before retiring from the court system in 2008. In 2018, Connie wrote *Hellfire in Hermantown*, a book about the impact of the 1918 Fire on her hometown.

C. Philip Johnson: After graduating from Esko in 1966, Phil earned a bachelor's degree in English from UMD, followed by a master's in 1978. He taught high school English in Finlayson and Proctor, retiring after 36 years. He and his wife Teri raised two sons and a daughter, all Esko graduates. He is the great-grandson of Nels (Naatus) Johnson, who arrived in Thomson Township in 1890.

Julie Kesti: Esko Class of 1973, Julie is a fourth-generation resident of Thomson Township. She is a graduate of the University of Minnesota, Minneapolis, with a degree in journalism. She has a master's degree in library and information science from UCLA. Julie worked as a librarian at UCLA and then at Sandia National Laboratories in Albuquerque, NM. She and her daughter Paige reside in Esko.

Ronald Sillanpa: A 1963 Duluth Denfeld graduate, Ron has been an Esko resident for more than 40 years. He graduated from Minnesota Duluth with a degree in business education. He served in the Navy for four years and in the Naval Reserve for 24 years. Ron was with the DM&IR Railway for 33 years before retiring in 2005. He and his late wife, Linda, raised a son and a daughter, both Esko graduates. During production of this book, he was president of the Esko Historical Society.

THE ESKO HISTORICAL SOCIETY

This book was published by the Esko Historical Society, a nonprofit founded in 1952 as the Finnish American Memorial Foundation. The name was changed to its present form in 1977.

The historical society is known primarily for its superbly maintained, eight-structure museum on West Highway 61, next to the Esko, Minnesota, Post Office. Operated by volunteers, the museum complex is open from 2 p.m. to 5 p.m. Sundays from June through August and at other times by appointment.

In 2017, the society also created a rotating exhibit in the entrance of the Thomson Town Hall, open from 9 a.m. to 4 p.m. Monday through Friday.

This is the second book published by the society. The first, *Esko's Corner, An Illustrated History of Esko and Thomson Township*, became available in January 2014. A 387-page coffee table book in hard cover and dust jacket, it continues to be sold via various Esko, Cloquet and Duluth vendors (see list at www.eskohistory.com). Order forms are also available on the website.

Persons interested in the 1918 Fire and its impact on Thomson Township may also listen to the memories of survivors or their descendants on a CD titled "Pioneer Memories; Thomson Township 1918." It was produced by past society president Ken Nynas and is available for $8 at most Esko commercial outlets where this book is sold or through the society's website.

The Society meets on the third Monday of each month at 1 p.m. at the town hall, but in the summer meetings are held at about 6 p.m. at the museum.

BIBLIOGRAPHY

"Barn Survived Fire, Served Community." *Finnish American Reporter.* October 2012.

Bohren, Bill. "The Awfullest Day of My Life." Undated. Esko Historical Society.

Carroll, Francis M. *Crossroads in Time: A History of Carlton County, Minnesota.* Cloquet, Minn.: Carlton County Historical Society, 1987.

Carroll, Francis M. and Franklin Raiter. *The Fires of Autumn; The Cloquet-Moose Lake Disaster of 1918.* St. Paul, Minn.: Minnesota Historical Society Press, 1990.

Esko's Corner, An Illustrated History of Esko and Thomson Township. Esko Historical Society, 2013.

Gramlich, Elvie Kinnunen. "A Sunnarborg Saga." Undated. Esko Historical Society.

Harney, Catherine. "1918 Fire Impressions." Written in 1970. Donated to Esko Historical Society, 2017, by Margaret Harney Pagano.

Harney Family History. Compiled by Harney family cousins. Unpublished: 1970 and 1971.

Ikola, Rodney "Pera Family History." 2018. Esko Historical Society.

Konu, Arvid. "The River was a Refuge." Ca. 2010. Esko Historical Society.

Lindquist, Robert. "Stories of Sophie (Lindquist) Johnson." 2018. Esko Historical Society.

Lumppio, Saima A. "Saima's Story, The Fire That Changed My Life." Esko Historical Society. Undated.

Manley, Lieut. J. R. Letter to Commanding Officer, 3d Bn. Minn. H.G. Northeast Minnesota Historical Center, Kathryn Martin Library, Archives.

Martin, Rachel. "Anna Dickie Olesen, Advocate for 1918 Fire Victims." *The Senior Reporter,* February and March, 2017.

Mattinen, John A. *History of the Thomson Farming Area.* Trans. by Richard Impola. Cloquet, Minn. Carlton County Historical Society, 2000.

Maxham, Glenn. *Hell Fire and Damnation…in the fires of 1918.* Duluth, Minn. Self-published, 2004.

Nelson, Charles A. Unpublished diaries, 1918-1936. Loaned by Jody Acers.

Nopola, Dr. J.E. "65 Years in One Home." *Lutheran Voice,* 1969.

Reponen, Gerald I. "Growing Up on the Farm." Unpublished manuscript. Esko Historical Society.

Saari, Clyde. "The Story of the Winterquists and the Schools of Thomson Township." 1959. Carlton County Historical Society.

Severson, John A. *Delivered With Pride, A Pictorial History of the Duluth, Winnipeg & Pacific.* Superior, Wis.: Savage Press, 2008.

Sunnarborg, John E. and Charles A. Nelson. Letter to members of Finnish Local Mutual Fire Insurance Company. 1919. Copy, Esko Historical Society.

Tuohy, Dr. E.L. Letter to Major R.M. Weaver, November 1, 1918. Northeast Minnesota Historical Center, Kathryn Martin Library, Archives.

Verified Claim against United States of America Railroad Administration. Copy, Esko Historical Society.

Wisuri, Marlene. "Fire Took Heavy Toll Among Ethnic Finns." Email March 2018.

BIBLIOGRAPHY

Websites

Ancestry.com: www.ancestry.com

Minnesota Historical Society: www.mnhs.org+

Nopeming Sanitorium: www.nopeming.com

Newspapers

Cloquet Pine Knot, Cloquet, Minnesota.

Duluth Herald, Duluth, Minnesota.

Duluth News Tribune, Duluth, Minnesota.

Interviews/Oral Recordings

Maralyn (Reponen) Frank, Louis Frederickson, Hilda Hakkarainen, Ray Hatinen, Virginia (Heine) Hatinen, Mamie Juntunen Hjulberg, Selma Ikola, Clifford Johnson, Glen Juntunen, "Kayo" (Leslie) Kesti, Dale Kinnunen, Donald Kinnunen, Eugene Lindquist, Tina Hakkarainen Pearson, Kay Perttula, Donald A. Pykkonen, Donald W. Pykkonen, Gerald Reponen, George Sunnarborg.

Supplemental Information Sources

Death records, Carlton County Courthouse; Thomson Township Board Minutes, 1919-1935

INDEX

INDEX

Index

INDEX

To order additional copies of

Thomson Township's
NIGHT OF TERROR
THE GREAT 1918 FIRE

Contact Savage Press by
visiting our webpage at
www.savpress.com
or see our Savage Press Facebook page.

Or call 218-391-3070
to place secure credit card orders.
mail@savpress.com

Discounts for bulk orders from groups or educational
organizations are available.

Books also may be ordered directly from
the Esko Historical Society.
See **www.eskohistory.com**.

Additionally, books will be sold at most Esko
businesses as well as at certain Cloquet outlets and
some Duluth bookstores.